BATHROOMS

DESIGNS FOR LIVING

BATHROOMS

DESIGNS FOR LIVING

Wanda Jankowski

MetroBooks

MetroBooks

An Imprint of Friedman/Fairfax Publishers

Library of Congress Cataloging-in-Publication Data

Jankowski, Wanda.

    Bathrooms: designs for living / by Wanda Jankowski.

       p.   cm.

    Includes index.

    ISBN 1-56799-458-X

    1. Bathrooms.   2. Interior decoration.   I. Title.

NK2117.B33J36   1997

747.7'8--dc21

97-13042

CIP

Editor: Francine Hornberger

Art Director: Kevin Ullrich

Designer: Meredith Miller

Photography Editors: Deidra Gorgos and Deborah Bernhardt

Production Manager: Jeanne Hutter

Color separations by Ocean Graphic International Company Ltd.
Printed in Singapore by KHL Printing Co Pte Ltd

1 3 5 7 9 10 8 6 4 2

For bulk purchases and special sales, please contact:
Friedman/Fairfax Publishers
Attention: Sales Department
15 West 26th Street
New York, NY 10010
212/685-6610 FAX 212/685-1307

Visit our website:
http://www.metrobooks.com

Acknowledgments

My thanks and appreciation go to Francine Hornberger
for recruiting me for this project and for her stunning editing
and managing of this book; to Michael Friedman Publishing Group,
which has proved itself to be professional in every way;
and to B. Leslie Hart for her outstanding willingness
to share her knowledge and for giving me not one,
but two career breaks.

CONTENTS

Developing a Personal Style

Like any other room in the home, the bathroom can be a haven of beauty and comfort, as well as a functional place, if you adapt the decor and details of the space to your personality and lifestyle. But how do you accomplish this? This book is filled with examples of how to use fixtures, surfacing materials, paint, wallcoverings, lighting, and accessories to create a beautiful, relaxing, enjoyable environment that efficiently serves all its functions.

Today's baths are truly multifunctional spaces designed to accommodate any number of needs. Those concerned with health and fitness may include exercise equipment, a steam bath, whirlpool, or sauna in the configuration of their bathroom.

Those interested in gardening and the beauty of nature can add window walls that allow outdoor vistas to be enjoyed from indoors, or can fill the space with an array of plants and flowers to maintain a revitalizing connection with nature.

The bathroom today has become a place to relax and unwind after a hectic day, reflected in the migration of accessories and furnishings from other rooms of the home such as candles, bookshelves and magazine racks, electronic equipment, and even upholstered furniture pieces and fireplaces. And luxurious conveniences, accessories, and finishing touches like towel warmers, floor heating systems, tanning tables, and miniwashers all serve to reinforce the bathroom's new image.

ABOVE: A hammered copper backsplash and copper sink are unusual choices for a bathroom, but add a touch of elegance when juxtaposed against a countertop created with striking cobalt blue tiles. The stained glass window behind ties these disparate elements together.

OPPOSITE: This eclectic, luxurious bath embodies the idea of a bathroom as a haven for relaxation. The coolness of stone in the enclosed shower is juxtaposed with the warmth of wood in the whirlpool surround. A built-in seat provides a comfortable resting place in the shower. An abundance of windows, plants on the ledge surrounding the tub, and garden outside create a nature-inspired decor. By night the space is well lit from both the recessed and concealed lighting in the circular ceiling dome.

Advances in technology and design have made it possible to implement safety options in your bath that don't look merely functional but can be decorative as well. Grab bars, rounded corners, safety glass, waterproof lighting fixtures, water temperature controls, and skid-resistant flooring are all readily available and affordable.

From lighting fixtures and cabinetry to floor tiles and countertops, the options for making your bath more than just a functional space are limited only by your budget and imagination. No matter what size your room or budget, you can express your lifestyle and tastes in your bathroom's conception and design. A tray hand-painted with delicate flowers, a crystal bud vase that captures a sprig of freesia, scented soaps piled high in a footed porcelain dish, a favorite piece of wall art, a lace curtain tied back with a tasseled cord —special touches like these can be incorporated in any bath, no matter the room's dimensions.

Stretch the limits of your imagination and discard preconceived notions when decorating and accessorizing your bath. Why put one mirror on the wall when four or five of varied sizes and frames can be eye-catchingly arranged and, at the same time, visually expand the size of the room? Extend the interior vista by painting details of a countryside scene on one wall. Enrich visual enjoyment of the space by adorning beams or columns with a faux marble finish.

Whether you are preparing to move into a new home, completely renovating your existing apartment or house, or just sprucing up your bath, this collection of beautiful and practical bathroom ideas will help you enrich your living environment.

❋

ABOVE: Handsome wood covers just about every surface in this bathroom—the tub surround, vanity, paneled walls, toilet seat—adding richness to the space. Powder blue draperies complement matching blue-and-gold wallpaper and continue the feeling of richness. The mirror-backed storage unit takes advantage of the ceiling height with its many glass shelves used to hold colognes and perfumes, as well as decorative accessories like the framed photograph and colorful boxes. The white tiled floor with green square inserts contrasts with the darkness of the wood.

ABOVE: A large bathroom provides a wealth of design opportunities—only in the largest bathroom setting can one include a set of antique furnishings and a fireplace. Here, the "garden" of flowers in the upholstery, wallcoverings, and draperies is balanced by the clean, simple, and yet rich look of the marble tiled floor and faux marble clawfoot bathtub. The vastness of the room is further emphasized by the large mirrored wall over the fireplace.

CHAPTER ONE

Small and Secondary Bathrooms

How to make the most of a small bathroom is a problem most home owners and renters face, whether they are decorating a standard-sized master bath, a powder room, or guest or child's bathroom. Many city dwellers reside in apartments with small, sometimes windowless bathrooms, while suburbanites may live in houses constructed a half century or more ago when rooms were built smaller.

There are many ways to disguise the size of a small bathroom and give the room the illusion of space, as this chapter will show. You may feel, however, that your small bathroom is not cramped but cozy, and instead of inventing tricks to hide its size, you may instead opt to capitalize on its charm.

To enlarge your space without knocking down walls, you can mirror all or part of a wall. Or, to free up surface area in the room,

angle a sink or shower into a corner, install a pedestal sink, or build medicine cabinets and storage closets into your walls instead of mounting them. Consider installing a pocket door instead of a door that cuts into available space by opening into the room.

Light, like mirrors, can also be used to increase the perceived size of a space. To use light to its best advantage, install clear glass shower doors. These will expand the room visually in a way that an opaque shower curtain in a dark color cannot. Installing skylights or additional windows, or using glass block can also be your solution. Glass block works wonderfully because it lets an enormous amount of light in while providing a privacy barrier—you can't clearly see through it. A whole wall in your bathroom can be replaced by glass block, or perhaps just one of your shower walls.

ABOVE: The interplay of shapes and textures gives this room visual interest. The marble sink surround is unusually shaped: the dropped semicircle front piece conceals the plumbing hardware. This curving is mimicked in the brass legs at the corners of the sink surround. Two-toned, neutral-colored walls and soft natural and artificial lighting complement the cold feel of marble. Gardenlike touches also help to soften the space.

OPPOSITE: This intricately carved mirror frame and vanity are set off by the sepia-toned, sponge-painted wall in this bathroom. Golden leaves beautifully embellish the triple-pronged wall sconces with fabric shades. The wainscoting is accented by dark and light borders. The wall-mounted artwork with picture light makes the room seem like a fine gallery. Brass fixtures and crystal accessories further enhance the elegant space.

Choosing light-colored paint, wallpaper, and surface materials or using small tiles on the walls and larger tiles on the floor will also help to visually expand the space. Uplighted high ceilings painted light colors will create a warm, comfortable atmosphere, as well as seem to give the space more height. You may extend the decor or color scheme of an adjacent bedroom or dressing area into the bath. By picking up on the decor of an adjacent room, the bathroom will appear larger.

Instead of worrying about how to make a small space seem larger, concentrate on enhancing its qualities. A master bath in a prewar building may have original tiles in good condition which lend a vintage charm to the space. Older homes often include rich details, such as intricately carved wood moldings. Ornate wall sconces or doorknobs that complement a pedestal sink and claw-foot tub may also be part of what already makes your small bath special.

The most pressing problem with small baths that cannot be solved through optical illusions is efficient storage. Clutter from an overstuffed medicine cabinet or unorganized vanity can easily get in the way of your performing routine tasks with ease. If there is limited space for cosmetics or toiletries in the bath, perhaps a makeup table positioned in a well-lit corner of the bedroom, where there is an accessible electrical outlet for hair dryer and curling iron, is the answer. Storing supplies in a hallway closet, adding a built-in to the hallway, skirting your vanity, or building a bathtub frame if space allows will help contain clutter.

❋

ABOVE: In this small area there is ample counter space on which to rest essentials—washcloth, soap, creams, toothbrushes—and even flowers in a glass vase. The curved shape of the sink surround frees up space on either side, adding a perception of larger scale to the small room. Built-in shelves and multiple towel bars are always great storage ideas, especially in small bathrooms. The large mirror above the sink visually "doubles" the square footage of the room while the off-white palette prevents the richly paneled half-wood walls from appearing too "heavy."

ABOVE: Unusual touches in this bathroom include the round mirror suspended in front of the window, the raised sink that gives the appearance of a freestanding bowl, and wall-mounted, porcelain-knobbed faucets and spout. The triangular countertop turns the small corner into necessary functional space in this small room and the built-in shelving area adds sparkle. There's even room for an often-overlooked yet much appreciated item in the bath—a wastebasket.

ABOVE: The rope design that encircles the white pedestal sink is repeated by a stenciled "rope" painted around the perimeter of this bathroom.
The wall sconces and classically framed mirror set the tone for the space and serve to soften the stark black-and-white tile and trim.
The colorful floral-patterned shower curtain (reflected in the mirror) brightens the room.

ABOVE: There's a lot going on in this little corner of a Victorian-inspired bathroom, but it's all pulled together through thoughtful planning. Wallpaper and a matching vanity skirt create energy and unity in the space and the careful placement of fixtures and accessories prevents the room from seeming too "busy." The same dark wood that encircles the window is picked up in the vanity and small shelving unit that is used to store and display objets d'art. A gilded frame around the mirror and framed fern leaves reinforce the Victorian spirit of the room.

ABOVE: Simple but effective accessories such as tall white candlesticks, a vase bursting with fresh flowers, and a classical bowl filled with potpourri with matching soap dish are decorative elements that don't clutter this tiny space. A stylish bentwood bench holds towels within arm's reach of the shower and, because it is so narrow, does not obstruct the walkway. The white walls, light marble countertops, and glass shower doors visually open the room that is awash with natural light during the day thanks to a large swing-open window.

❧

ABOVE: A profusion of mirrors helps to make this tiny bath look larger and imbues the room with an eclectic visual interest: the simple, functional mirror above the sink counters the regal, gold-framed mirror above the toilet. The charm of the space is further revealed in trompe l'oeil details: maintenance-free "curtains" painted on the wall behind the toilet and the garden scene behind matching painted curtains on the opposite wall (reflected in the mirror).

OPPOSITE: Mirrors, mirrors everywhere! This is one of the most effective ways to make a small bath look larger and add character at the same time. Whether they are flea market finds or heirlooms handed down from past generations, framed or unframed, round, oval, or rectangular, etched or beveled, mirrors can be particularly effective reflecting daylight in a room with ample windows. In this bath, large windows open out onto the garden, continuing the feeling of openness.

ABOVE LEFT: A well-equipped guest bathroom will make your visitor feel at home. In this space, matching containers for shaving items, makeup brushes, and Q-Tips, and hooks to hang robes or dressing gowns show a keen attention to detail. Fresh flowers in tall silver vases complete the welcoming feeling.

ABOVE RIGHT: This bath proves that functional rooms don't have to be sterile and unexpressive. Like any room in the home, the bathroom can reflect the personality of the owner, the locale in which the house is situated, or the period in which the house was built. In this quaint bath, interest is achieved by combining disparate elements. The aged-looking, diagonally paneled walls and the "tree branch" curtain rod give this bathroom a warm, natural feel which is complemented by a crystal-laden chandelier and the silver accessories on the tank and shelf. Porcelain fittings, the grooming mirror on a swing arm, and an old clock on the shelf are reminiscent of a bygone era.

ABOVE: Floral wallpaper provides just the right touch of color and pattern in this white bath. A textured tile border in the shower breaks up the white ceramic tiles without introducing more color. The glistening brass fixtures and fittings imbue the space with elegance. Perhaps the most interesting observation about this bathroom is its perceived size. At first glance, it looks like a large and luxurious space, but on closer inspection, it is discovered that it is only an illusion: the closet on the opposite end of the room is mirrored from top to bottom and seems to double the size of the space.

ABOVE: A high ceiling opens this narrow room. The rectangular dimensions are played upon throughout the space in the highly vertical doorway of the circular shower and the aluminum-framed window. Countering these vertical planes are the horizontal countertop with an oval inset and long mirror above. Unusual in a bathroom, wood flooring and cabinetry are fitting additions and create a contrast to the cool marble shower wall and countertop.

TIPS ON STORAGE AND DISPLAY

To make your bathroom a more efficient space, take time to think through where the best places are to store grooming and hygiene items, and how to maintain the working order of the room. Here are some suggestions for storage and display:

▨ Put racks or drawers into the undersink cabinet rather than using it as an unorganized catchall.

▨ Install robe hooks behind the bathroom door. Attach a rack for shampoos, conditioners, hair spray, and soaps within your shower.

▨ A conventional door needs room to swing open. In a small bath, consider installing a pocket door that slides into a wall when not needed. This will free up space for a rack, shelves, a small table, or art.

▨ Conceal your wastebasket inside the vanity cabinet to lessen clutter.

▨ If space is limited, keep only items you use every day in the bathroom. Store extras and what you occasionally use in an adjacent dressing area or hall closet. Similarly, you may opt to place a dressing table and clothes hamper in the bedroom rather than trying to perform grooming tasks in a very small bathroom.

▨ Mount a magazine rack or shelf to the side of the bathtub to make reading materials easily accessible.

▨ A cabinet above the toilet can hold cleansers and replacement items, such as an extra box of tissues or rolls of toilet paper.

▨ Built-in cabinets and closets make for a sleek-looking bathroom. Besides drawers and shelves, they can also conceal a small washer and dryer.

▨ Open shelves or niches above the tub or toilet can display towels, plants, and decorative accessories.

▨ The windowsill is ideal for "storing" plants, affording a bit of privacy from the outside and easy to maintain if it is covered with ceramic tile or a slab of marble or granite.

▨ Create a long shelf between the tub and the wall for bath salts, sponges and soap dishes, as well as for candles to create a relaxing mood.

▨ Built-in niches are great for fresh flowers, large seashells, or other beautiful items. For dramatic effect, set a small halogen spotlight recessed into the top of the niche to highlight the objects displayed.

In this bath, the lack of existing storage options prompted the owners to bring in furnishings from other rooms in the home—a wood shelving unit and a chest of drawers.

❋

ABOVE: The unusual antique map wallpaper in this bathroom, along with the tall narrow bookcase stacked with books beside the toilet, invites dreaming of faraway places. The lanternlike sconce lends a nautical feel and continues the adventure theme while a gold-framed mirror and upswept curtain behind the toilet add a refined air.

ABOVE LEFT: A masculine look is achieved in this tiny wood-paneled room. The heaviness of the wood is relieved by the simple diamond pattern in the black-and-white tile floor and the white-painted walls and ceiling above the panels. Ample storage is provided by a glass-doored built-in cabinet adjacent to the classic pedestal sink. Part of the appeal of this room comes from the inclusion of personal treasures—a model ocean liner, a sexy porcelain bathing beauty, and, of course, a rubber ducky!

ABOVE RIGHT: Charming details abound in this small, circular powder room. The sink is made to look like an old-fashioned porcelain wash basin with painted blue flowers. Plumbing is cleverly concealed by wooden legs and shelving. Bold green and white stripes enliven the wall from chair-rail height. Lighting is provided by two lanternlike sconces and a ceramic overhead pendant fixture.

OPPOSITE: What may have been destined to become a closet or storage nook instead became this interesting bathroom that looks carved out from under the staircase. Rough stone walls and an abundance of wood lend a rustic flair. The stone sink surround and candle-bulbed wall sconce reinforce the cavelike appeal.

OPPOSITE: Natural light flooding in from two windows in this bath gives the room an airy feeling. An unusual beadboard-paneled tub surround is as attractive as it is useful—its wide ledges are home to bathing supplies as well as an array of plants. A wooden chair with a straw seat and straw roll-up blinds are the perfect complement to the all-natural theme of the room.

ABOVE: A framed turn-of-the-century advertisement and the antique look of the tub and sink fixtures give this bath a decidedly nostalgic flavor. The exposed-beam ceiling (as seen in the top left corner of the mirror) combined with the matching vanity and framed windows and mirror gives the room a rustic elegance. Modern-day conveniences—a cool stone tub surround and stainless steel sink—don't take away from the design.

ABOVE LEFT: Trompe l'oeil curtains painted in soft blue and white mimic the look of real ones in this high-ceilinged bath and free up limited wall space for a small mirror and personal items—a vase with flowers, a framed photograph, and sculpture. Privacy is maintained with simple white shades.

ABOVE RIGHT: Black-and-white motifs can sometimes seem austere—but not when penguins are involved. This bevy of birds decorating the shower curtain evokes a sense of fun and playfulness. A stepped divider separates the sink from the tub area while providing an interesting display opportunity. Double towel racks are conveniently mounted at shower and at bathing height.

OPPOSITE: Harmonious elements combine in this room making what could have been an awkward, tiny space into a welcoming one. The sloped ceiling is hardly noticed, overshadowed as it is by beautiful leaded glass windows. The shorter wall is utilized by towel racks and sliding door cabinets. Simple country style accents—the small rocking chair, the metal horse frozen in mid-gallop, wooden medicine cabinet—all play up the quaint elements of the space. Baskets are great receptacles for towels, sponges, and toiletries, both on the floor and above the tub.

ABOVE: The numerous elements of this bathroom are all unified through various shades of yellow and gold in the tiles and the upper walls. Classical-styled pedestals serve double duty by providing storage space for towels and bath accessories under the sink in a room with limited storage potential as well as making a strong design statement.

ABOVE: A sleek and narrow wood-based vanity and complementary streamlined mirror are neatly tucked away into a corner alcove of this bathroom. The sponge-painted walls allow for the rest of the design to remain sparse. All that is needed to complete the decor is a vase of fresh flowers and a seashell.

OPPOSITE: This urban apartment bathroom achieves a fresh, cool feel through marble tile. Added elegance comes from the wood-paneled and painted bathtub surround. Built-in shelving above the tub provides an ideal storage space for towels or bath accessories without compromising space. At the foot of the bath, a built-in shelf is designed to hold bath salts, soaps, and, when the mood permits, candles. Since privacy is not a concern in this high-rise bathroom, curtains are not required, keeping views accessible while making the room appear larger.

ABOVE: Maintaining old-fashioned charm is one way to de-emphasize the size of a small bath. A Victorian theme comes across in this room through a beadboard wainscot, pedestal sink, and claw-foot tub with freestanding showerhead. The detailed metalwork on the radiator further radiates Victorian style. Delicately patterned wallpaper, matching curtains, and floor in the same powder blue tone bring the room together. The curtain rod and holder both feature a favorite Victorian motif—nature.

ABOVE: A small space can be an elegant space, as evidenced here. A lovely striped valance complements the peach-toned bull-nosed countertop set slightly into the wall. The inset is covered with a large mirror that increases the perception of spaciousness. The small pleated shades on the wall sconces soften the room, and the brass fittings and decorative box add a bit of sparkle. Towels are conveniently hung on racks mounted on the cabinet front below the sink.

OPPOSITE: An exotic atmosphere was created in this powder room with sponge-painted walls and a hand-painted vanity with matching mirror. Accessories, including a cluster of hats, are unobtrusive in the small, narrow room. Recessed lighting softens the glow of the overhead hanging pendant fixture.

✻

ABOVE: Large windows in this garden-level apartment bring nature indoors. Mother Nature herself has provided a substitute for the window treatments that are normally needed to ensure privacy. A built-in niche above the tub is ideal for storage of towels, or for use as a display area for flowers or personal possessions—always a bonus in a small space.

ABOVE LEFT: Sometimes even a small bathroom can accommodate all of the modern comforts and conveniences—in this case, it includes a bidet. This bathroom has a Southwestern feel with its sand-colored, sponge-painted walls and complementary terra-cotta floor tiles. The clever mirror simulates the look of a window, enlarging the space two-fold.

ABOVE RIGHT: A vanity with drawers of different sizes is a perfect addition to any bathroom, as the items stored therein come in various shapes and sizes. By storing prescription and over-the-counter medication and toothbrush and toothpaste in higher drawers, hair products and makeup in middle drawers, and hairdryer and curling iron below, the need for a separate medicine cabinet has been eliminated in this small bath.

ABOVE: This pool house makes effective use of limited space. The open shower is just a few steps away from the bed, but remains separate. Icy blue tiles mimic both the color and texture of water. There is a built-in niche for soap and sponge, and a flexible handheld showerhead. After a dip in the pool outside, the bather simply walks through the glass-paneled door and steps into the shower.

OPPOSITE: A wall of windows distracts from the compact size of this bathroom. Because of the home's secluded location, window treatments are not necessary for privacy. The routine of bathing and grooming tasks is minimized for the user of this space, who experiences around the clock different aspects of nature—blazing sunshine, a gentle rainfall, or the mellowing onset of dusk. The low shower stall is easy to step into, and the complementary surround at the base of the mirror wall is ideal for resting soap and shampoo.

OPPOSITE: The personality of the owner of this bathroom really comes across in the decor. Colorful paintings are arranged seemingly at random on walls. Mirrors of different sizes and shapes and collectibles also hang from the bubblegum pink walls.

ABOVE: The absence of a vanity on this Victorian pedestal sink and a wood-framed mirror that is almost as long as the wall from which it hangs, in addition to an oversize window, open up this narrow space. The white-tiled lower portion of the wall, floor, and white ceiling break up the intensity of the striped wallpaper with black trim.

ABOVE: Positioning a sink and vanity in the corner of a room frees up space for storage on either side. A mirror above the longer side of the vanity reflects the window on the adjacent wall, creating the illusion of another window. The wallpaper border draws the eye up to the uplighted white ceiling, making the room seem more spacious. Personal touches add warmth—a golden-framed drawing propped up beneath the window, photos, an antique jewelry chest, a wooden Stegosaurus, and a vase filled with fresh flowers.

OPPOSITE: Romantic touches that give this bath an interesting character include the fanlight window with spiderweb mullions, the antique planter, and a miniature chair tucked under the pedestal sink. The mirror is treated like artwork—framed beautifully with a wall-mounted picture light above it. Plenty of storage for extra towels and books is provided in the narrow, multishelved rack.

CHAPTER TWO

Large and Luxurious Spaces

A large bathroom presents its own set of design challenges. The layout needs to be planned to make everything readily accessible—which is difficult when there is an abundance of available space. Also important, of course, the room needs to look well designed.

The decor of a large en suite bath may be a continuation of the design of the master bedroom. Furniture may make its way into a large master bath—from ornate, hand-painted dressing screens to armchairs and chaise longues. Attention to detail contributes to the visual enjoyment of any room, and the bath is no different. Large spaces are ideal for wood accents, painted borders and patterns, contemporary patterned tile work, or hand-painted porcelain basins. Display areas for cherished objects or

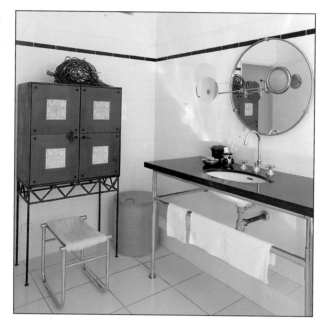

floral arrangements in glass and crystal, lidded jars for holding grooming or makeup aids, and potpourri containers are all easily accommodated in a large bathroom.

Large baths also allow for more options in lighting. Task lighting at the sink for cleansing the face, applying makeup, or shaving can be switched on separately from mood-creating decorative sconces located elsewhere in the room. Lighting dimmers are a simple way to change the look and mood of a room with the touch of a switch.

Additionally, large baths provide owners with possibilities they may not have even considered for the bath. Baths designed as sunrooms or miniconservatories filled with plants bring the feeling of nature and the outdoors inside the home. A blending of exteriors and interiors also occurs

ABOVE: This bath has a sleek and streamlined modern feel thanks to a black lacquer countertop mounted on a chrome base and sophisticated chrome fixtures. A bench that tucks away under a storage cabinet and chrome mirror complete the effect. The beige storage cabinet softens the decor while serving as a much needed storage receptacle in the sparse room.

OPPOSITE: In this large space, a partial wall was built to separate the toilet and bidet from the bathing area. Unbathlike furnishings imbue the room with a romantic feel but maintain functionality. A freestanding wood and glass cabinet holds towels and objets d'art. A simple pedestal supports a lush plant while a sponge holder that looks like an oversized cocktail glass is a good idea for keeping bath items in plain view.

when large windows or doors open onto private gardens beyond. Saunas and steam baths help to create a kind of tropical paradise in the home. In some instances, entertainment centers can be included in the large bath, equipped with a tape or CD player and a small television for watching weather reports and the news while getting ready for work.

The large and luxurious bathroom is a place where a couple can relax at the end of the day. Tubs, whirlpools, hot tubs, and showers built for two can be supplemented by a warming fireplace and over-sized comfy pillows scattered before it. A nearby bar area with a minirefrigerator is perfect for stocking wine, mineral water, or other special treats.

The most pressing concern you'll have when decorating your bath is making sure that your large bathroom is an efficient space. Plan cabinetry so all the items you need for grooming are located in one area in the room, cleaning supplies in another, towels and linens in yet another. By grouping like objects together, you'll save time that may have been wasted before trying to locate things in a vast space.

ABOVE: The luxury of space has allowed the owners of this bath to tuck a whirlpool into its own secluded corner. By day, natural light pours into the room through an abundance of windows. A double band of blue tile on the walls, echoed in the color of the his-and-her sinks, serves to unify the room. A cabinet built into the wall right next to the sink provides a place to tuck toiletries within easy access of the sink without occupying too much space.

OPPOSITE: An oriental dressing screen forms a rich backdrop to the circular table where both decorative and functional items rest. Tufted curtains enhance the large window and let in plenty of daylight. A matching curtain visually separates the tub from the toilet area, creating privacy for the bather. Plants, colorful towels hung on both sides of the pedestal sink, and accessories with a Far-Eastern feel give this room an exotic appeal.

OPPOSITE: Large enough to be a living room, sunroom, and bath combined, this bathroom is like a summer resort. The greenhouse windows are covered with shades to ensure privacy and block out the sun's glare. Bamboo tables and palm trees continue the tropical theme of the room.

ABOVE: Beautiful stonework walls and lush green plants create the illusion of a jungle setting in this luxurious bathroom. The vanity area is amply lit by several bulbs while track lighting units over the tub can be adjusted to highlight plants or displays or set a mood. Windows everywhere and skylights complete the illusion of bathing in a tropical paradise.

ABOVE: Where better is there to place a whirlpool than adjacent to a large deck? Plenty of adjustable windows provide good ventilation and there is recessed lighting for nighttime use of the tub. An iron bar separates the recessed jacuzzi area from the rest of the space.

OPPOSITE: Taking a shower in this bathroom is like showering under a rain forest waterfall. The shower's extra large head provides a luxurious spray of water. All-glass walls provide plenty of natural light, while greenery everywhere ensures privacy.

ABOVE: A vast expanse of custom cabinetry provides a place for everything in this enormous bathroom. Soft-toned pink marble floors, faux marble cabinet faces, and off-white walls and ceiling frame the vibrant greenery in view beyond the large windows. The window seat provides a place to relax and enjoy the surroundings while underneath presents a functional storage unit. Vanities for her and him are easily accommodated in this spacious room.

ABOVE: The wood steps and tub surround, the chandelier, the wall-hung artwork, and the classical columns make this whirlpool area look more like a study than a bathroom. An unusually placed chandelier with fabric shades hangs directly over the tub. A stylish brass clothes rack in the form of a man holds towels and bathrobe within easy reach of the bather. The gleaming brass hardware has been installed on the side of the tub instead of at the head so it does not obstruct the bather from getting into the tub.

✦

ABOVE: Wood flooring in combination with a double-door closet, flowing draperies, detailed moldings, chair, and small table makes this area seem decidedly unbathroomlike—as if it were another room in the house. A small window in one of the shower walls lets in light from the windowed room beyond, while the bull-nosed edged marble countertop and the marble shower walls add richness to the space. Fresh flowers liven up the room.

ABOVE: The archway above the alcove tub is echoed in the arched window overlooking the garden, making it the focal point in this neutral-toned bath. An oversized ottoman, occasional table, and antique chair give the functional space a touch of elegance. Always a plus in a large bathroom, ample storage of grooming items and personal mementos is provided by a vanity chock full of drawers.

ABOVE LEFT: A skylight was installed in this bathroom to combat the effect of the sloped ceiling. The mirrored wall behind the shower bounces light coming in from the skylight through the clear-glass shower door. A double vanity and storage closets are easily accommodated here. The ceiling is whimsically painted with trompe l'oeil suns and stars, contributing to the open feeling of the space. A mosaic box stores jewelry and keepsakes as well as provides a splash of color.

ABOVE RIGHT: The first thing you notice in this large double bathroom area is the dark green tiles "raining down" the walls below the slightly curved ceiling in the shower area. Multilevel towel bars and a small closet are ideal for storing robes or exercise attire. The second part of the room contains the vanity and repeats the cascading tile pattern. A whirlpool tub is built into the floor for easy access.

OPPOSITE: Sharp angles and sleek curves provide visual interest in this bath. The ribbed, round brass sink set in a curved marble vanity is only one of many elegant touches. Soffits are complemented by angled mirror panels at the sink and grooming area countertops. Recessed lighting creates illumination for more function-oriented tasks while uplights concealed in the soffits cast a golden glow onto the yellow-painted coved ceiling, creating a feeling of warmth.

ABOVE: Dark wood paneling, black countertops, the black and peeling ivory chair, and the seascape artwork come together to impart a nautical feel in this large bathroom. A light-colored floor tile, as well as light wood cabinets and off-white upper walls and vaulted ceiling lighten the room. Towel warming bars are a luxurious touch. The large shower is easily illuminated: the clear glass shower and small interior window allow for a generous amount of light to pass through.

ABOVE: The dramatic use of black and white makes a striking statement in this luxurious deco-influenced bathroom. Richly paneled black cabinetry is topped with a white marble countertop that matches the faux marble floor, walls, and bathtub and serves to cool the space while a cream-colored door and carpet reintroduce warmth. The grooming area of the mirrored wall is broken up by a medicine cabinet delineated by an arresting black outline and hidden by a gauzy white curtain. The fixtures and tub fitting are all—unusually—black. The bathtub's wide ledge provides plenty of space on which to rest sponges, soaps, and personal accessories.

ABOVE: In this bathroom, the draped shower curtain follows the contour of the slanted ceiling, creating a dramatic effect. An abundance of counter space adjacent to the sink (a plus in an oversized bathroom) allows for the easy performance of grooming tasks. The soft lighting of a desk lamp, the warmth of an area rug, and traditionally styled chairs at the vanity and next to the bathtub create a homey feel.

ABOVE: In this spacious bath, a buttery palette, hardware-free drawers in the white vanity, a mirrored wall, and a smooth polished marble floor are a subtle backdrop for classical accents such as the painting that draws the eye up to the high ceiling and the enormous etched glass window. Towels are cleverly stored in light wicker baskets around the bathtub while a three-tiered hammered steel piece holds soaps.

TIPS ON WORKING WITH A PROFESSIONAL

Whether you seek out a contractor, interior designer, or Certified Bath Designer to help you create your dream bath, remember that it's your bath they are designing. These professionals will contribute their expertise and answer many questions you may have, but it is your responsibility to come to them with as clear an idea as possible of what kind of bathroom you want. Professionals can only fulfill your dreams if you tell them what your dreams are! Here are tips on how to prepare for your meeting.

※ Collect examples of what you do and do not like from home design magazines, newspapers, and other photo sources and sketch the solutions you find there. Tour showhouses and model homes.

※ Think about how you use your bath and how you would like to use it if you could change the space. Write down all the ways you and other people in your household use it. List preferences for showers and baths and times they are taken.

※ Make note of any problems or inconveniences you have with your current bath. Is there too little storage? Is there not enough ventilation? Is the lighting too dim in certain parts of the room? Are too many family members regularly kept waiting to use it?

※ Make a list of what you'd like to have in your bath that you don't have now. Then prioritize the list, so the professional knows what you would most like to have if all of your requests aren't achievable.

※ Put function first. No matter how wonderful a fixture or material looks, if it doesn't serve a useful purpose, your eventual displeasure will outweigh its aesthetic appeal. Think about traffic patterns, adequate storage, and ample lighting.

※ Establish a budget and stick to it. Few people can afford *everything* they really want. Your wish lists and priorities, with the guidance of a professional, will help you choose what to purchase.

※ When it comes to style and decor, draw clues about your preferences from your other possessions and environments. Think about the kinds of objects you collect or artwork you own. What are your favorite colors? What colors come up most in your clothing and in the other rooms in your home? What styles, lines, and kinds of prints are best for you?

※ Be flexible. If you would like marble but can't afford it, perhaps another material can give you the look of marble. Be open to substitutions that might achieve your goal in a different—even better—way than you originally imagined.

※ Be open-minded: welcome creative or innovative ideas. Experiment with mixing and matching textures, colors, and materials.

※ You don't have to have your entire home redone to seek the services of a professional designer. Many have fee structures that accommodate "one-room wonders."

※ How do you find a professional? Ask neighbors, friends, co-workers, and architects and builders you trust who they would recommend. And when you contact the professional, ask for and examine carefully the entire portfolio—not just one project. Then ask for and check out the professional's references.

※ Remember that it is important to establish a rapport with the designer. He or she is there to make your vision a reality, not to create a vision of their own. Clear communication between you and the consultant is key.

※ Ask questions about the fee structure: is there an hourly rate or a design fee that covers the entire project? Find out if purchases and expenses are treated separately. Some designers require a retainer with the signed contrast to ensure that the client is serious. Negotiate a payment schedule that serves you both.

※ Ask plenty of questions along the way—it's up to you to know what's going on, and to supervise the work as it proceeds to make sure you are getting what you were promised.

ABOVE: The picture of luxury, the size of this his-and-her bathroom even allows it to accommodate a center island replete with towel warmers and cabinets for storage. The tub is set within a semicircular alcove marked by a large curved window, giving it a sense of separateness from the rest of the bath. The marble ledge surrounding the bathtub itself is an ideal resting place for soaps and sponges or votive candles to create a romantic mood.

❋

OPPOSITE: This large bathroom in a small living space is sided on one end by the kitchen and by the living room on the other. Meant for a single person, the bath is wide open. Cabinets under the stairs are custom-designed as drawers and storage units.

❋

ABOVE: Form and function are nicely combined in this space-age bath. The frosted glass storage unit that rests on the tub surround separates the bathing area from the toilet and allows the user to see what's inside while protecting the contents from splashing water. Plastic hooks on the side hold robes and towels. The shower curtain serves double duty as a privacy curtain when drawn across the toilet area. Three playful lighting fixtures on the far wall prevent the long windowless room from looking dark and cavernous.

ABOVE: Spending an evening at home takes on a new meaning in a bathroom fitted with a fireplace and plenty of comfy pillows. The focal point of the room is the tub with its curvy shape mimicked above in the ceiling soffit. Art objects including sculptures and a gilded mirror as well as plants personalize the space. Plenty of vanity storage space, a separately enclosed shower, and a view of the garden outside make this bath one in which it would be easy to spend time.

OPPOSITE: This large bath is awash with eclectic elements and a 1940s elegance: a wood-paneled ceiling replete with skylight, green marble floor and vanity countertop, and pink marble tub platform. The visual richness is enhanced by the sparkling brass frame around the shower panels and etched-glass windows.

OPPOSITE: This bath area brings the outdoors inside with a decklike floor and a row of glass doors and panels that presents infinite vistas. The large tub is surrounded by luscious white marble and separated from other areas of the bath by a low black marble partition. Uplight from concealed cove lighting highlights the wood ceiling beams. A large makeup counter is supported by custom cabinetry that provides ample storage for accessories.

ABOVE LEFT: The sleek, brown marble floor tiles and rich wood paneling set the tone of the decor in this bath. The extensive use of knotted wood panels not only on the walls but in the ceiling beams and sloping roof creates a saunalike feel. Lighting is provided by high angled windows that also maintain privacy.

ABOVE RIGHT: A gloriously arched etched glass window floods this decidedly unbathroom-like space with natural light during the day, and serves to further the room's vastness. A complementary etched glass window lets light into the shower. The wood, marble-topped vanity and table lamp make the room feel more like a bedroom than a bath.

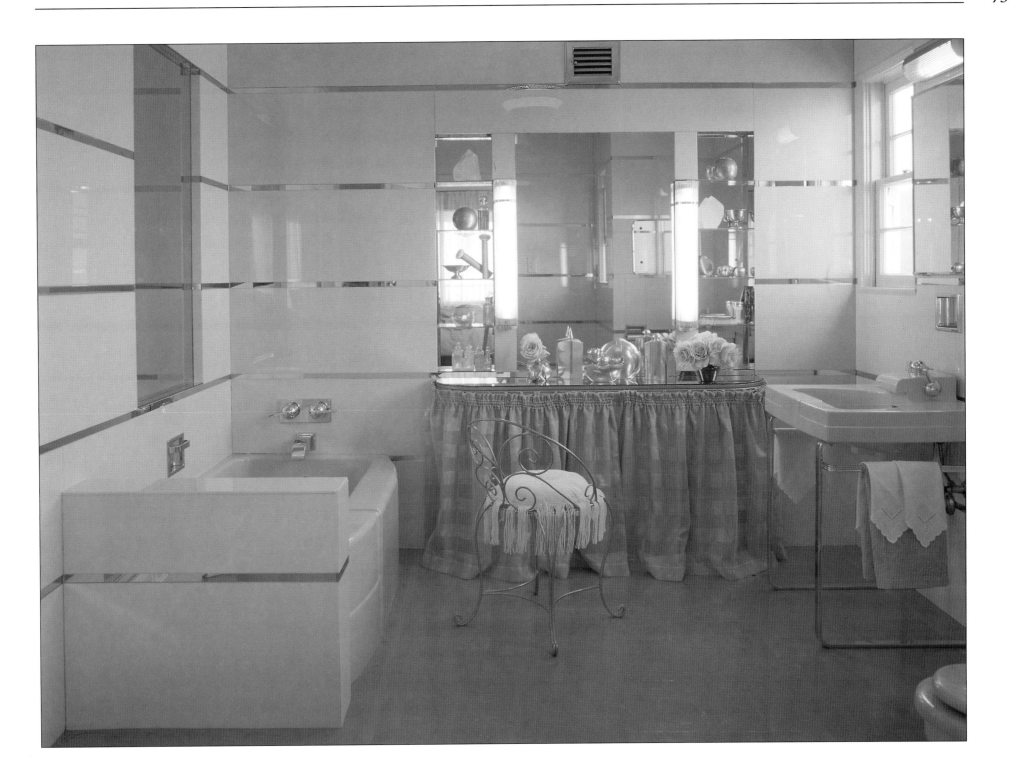

OPPOSITE: This his-and-her bath is an extension of the master bedroom, as reflected in the glass doors of the large mirrored closets. The enormous skylight floods the room with natural light. The light beige walls and floor as well as the generous use of wood further brighten the space, which is large enough to accommodate a couple of rocking chairs and lush greenery.

ABOVE: Mirror stripes unify this basically white bath. Natural lighting is enhanced by a wall fixture above the sink mirror, vertical sidelighting fixtures at the vanity, and a decorative pendant for general lighting in the center of the room. The gathered fabric skirt on the makeup table and curvy metal chair add a feminine touch to the space.

❋

ABOVE: The freestanding tub in this room recalls the turn of the century, but is much larger than any tub back then would have been. White-painted bead-board paneling, a Victorian wall sconce, a pedestal-legged white table, and ruffled chair continue the nostalgic feeling. The built-in storage space on the side of the vanity is accessed by a charming tasseled pull. Sleek marble floor tiles and marble vanity countertop along with chrome vases atop the counter bring the feeling of another style—art deco—into the room.

❁

ABOVE: An eclectic flavor permeates this bath with a leopard print cushion on a gilded stool and stylized patterned rug and trunk. An extra ledge on the tub surround is a great keeper of soaps, candles, and decorative elements like a pair of wooden boxes, oriental vase, and model ship. The unusually mullioned windows are shaded at the bottom to allow in daylight while maintaining privacy for the bather. A telephone and radio have been included for convenience.

CHAPTER THREE

Paint and Wallcoverings

Decorative wall treatments are an effective way to enhance or change the look of your bath. Through the magic of paint, wallpaper, wood paneling, tiles, or even hanging fabric, an ordinary bathroom can become an extraordinary haven.

Paint can be used in several ways, including coating walls in a solid color and implementing decorative paint techniques. Painting a room with light colors will make it appear larger, and a ceiling seem higher. Dark colors will create a more intimate space and, when mixed with other rich materials like wood moldings, can provide a very elegant look.

In trompe l'oeil, greatly detailed images are painted on surfaces to deceive the eye. A painted-on garden path lined with flowers can brighten your bath on even the coldest winter day. Or, if your powder room is too small for the elaborate, classical styled draperies you wish to hang, you can paint them on. A windowless bath can be transformed with the addition of a trompe l'oeil window that looks out onto a lush green valley or an orchard replete with birds and small animals.

Stenciling is one of the most popular home decorating techniques today. Adding a stenciled border where walls meet the ceiling will make a room seem larger because the pattern draws the eye up. Or, in a very high-ceilinged space, a pattern can be stenciled around the perimeter of the room at shoulder level to change the scale of the room. Stenciling is also an inexpensive way to repeat the patterns contained in your floor tiles or accessories to unify the space.

Hand-painted tiles are available from most tile manufacturers. These will add color and pattern to a space while performing a

ABOVE: If you don't have a window or a beautiful view outside your bathroom window, create one with trompe l'oeil. No matter how harsh the weather conditions outside, this bather will always be able to enjoy a beautiful springtime image of scenic rolling green hills and a winding blue river!

OPPOSITE: This bath is awash in opulent details including a mosaic laurel pattern inset in the marble floor and a curved rich wood-paneled bathtub with silver classical ornamentation. The gold columns behind the tub and the painting continue the classical theme. The barreled sponge-painted ceiling recalls the splendor of an ancient palace. Lighting is provided by recessed fixtures and two candlelike sconces at either end of the massive tub.

necessary function. Whether used to decorate an entire wall or as a delicate border treatment, tiles in florals, abstract or geometric shapes, or images that reflect the work of your favorite artist can personalize your bath in a medium that is relatively permanent and easy to maintain.

Sponge painting, ragging, and combing are some of the other decorative paint techniques you may try. These call for more paint and effort than some of the other techniques, but the outcome can be very rewarding. Each of these is worked by applying several layers of paint and then partially removing the outer layers with either a sponge, a rag, or a comb to expose the layers underneath.

Other popular wallcoverings encompass a wide range of materials from water-resistant papers to fabrics like sheer or lace curtains to elaborately patterned draperies, wood paneling, marble, slate, stone, brick, and mosaic tile. Chapter four will more closely examine the use of these special materials.

Painted surfaces and wallcoverings need to be evaluated in the space in which they will be used. Some baths contain glass-block insets, stained or leaded glass panels, or large window walls. There may be a lot of daylight in the bath or perhaps electric light is the main source of illumination. Consider your main light source. Do the fixtures contain incandescent bulbs that play up warm red and yellow tones, or fluorescent tubes that may emphasize cooler shades of blue and green? This can determine which color is best for your bath.

Be sure to examine what kinds of wall treatments are best suited for wet versus dry areas in the bath. When planning your bathroom's decorating scheme, investigate how water-resistant your choice of paints and wallpapers are and, most importantly, if they will hold up to steam and humidity.

ABOVE: Painted flowers climb to the top in this extraordinarily high-ceilinged bathroom, and used in combination with the ceiling's exposed wood beams and garden views, give this room a feeling of oneness with nature. The polished wood vanity, pristine white floors draped with elegant area rugs, a classical pedestal topped with a white porcelain pitcher serving as a vase for fresh flowers, and wicker chaise longue make this space feel more like a bedroom or living room than a bathroom.

OPPOSITE: This bathroom shows an outrageous use of trompe l'oeil. Walls and ceiling are abloom with a whimsical garden scene just beyond the painted stone "walls" that envelop the bath. A vase of flowers has been painted over the toilet tank and seems as if it's actually resting there. A garden gate opening onto a path beneath a flower-filled trellis is an invitation to another world.

ABOVE LEFT: A charming hand-painted border separates the soft yellow top portion of this wall from the sponge-painted orange lower portion. An unusual wooden triangular shelving unit holds a colorful array of towels—a decorative device in itself.

ABOVE RIGHT: This bath experiments with a variety of painting techniques simultaneously. The bottom section of the wall is sponge painted a warm brown and is separated from the top with a hand-painted crisscross border. Imagery of the Wild West is painted on the top portion of the walls, establishing a Western theme. Rugs and towels were chosen to complement the painted walls. An optical illusion, the back of the door almost "disappears" because it is painted exactly the same as the walls.

OPPOSITE: A hand-stenciled border can do wonders for a plain white room. In this bathroom, with its wood molding and plaid curtains, the effect is of a country retreat. Framed sepia-toned prints of historic buildings complete the quaint charm.

ABOVE: A powder blue paper with bouquets of white flowers covers the top portion of the walls and the ceiling of this stylish bathroom, creating a cocoonlike effect. The lower walls have been painted to achieve a pearl-like appearance. Victorian features like the claw-foot tub and pedestal sink and mirror, as well as the lighting fixtures and the silk, tasseled pillow at the side of the tub give the feeling of being in another time, as do lightly painted flowers on the exposed wood floor.

ABOVE: Here the imagination has been allowed to run wild in the quotes and pictures inscribed onto the gray-painted walls. An above-ground whirlpool bath offers a place to ponder the images and find new inspirations. Display niches have been cleverly created under the steps to the whirlpool to display objets d'art.

ABOVE: This bathroom gracefully re-creates an Italian villa. A slight step down from the long curtained windows brings one into an open space rich with lovely details and a creamy palette. An intricate pattern was stenciled on the window above the tub, creating the illusion of a garden trellis. The tub surround is also graced by a stenciling treatment—in this case a bouquet of flowers that seems to have been picked from the wall. The paneled ceiling is complemented by a simple iron and glass chandelier.

OPPOSITE: A sprig of delicate foliage seems to run up the wall from the pristine white tub. The walls themselves are a work of art. A marbling technique has been ingeniously achieved with pink, gray, and lavender paint and gives the room a sense of texture. And look closely: diamond shapes subtly line the walls. The whole effect is complemented by beautifully framed mirrors in the room's palette.

OPPOSITE: Decorative painting abounds in this bathroom. Lime green walls are enhanced by hand-painted tiles and the overall effect is that of a garden in the springtime. An "area rug" of bright flowers was hand-painted on the floor tiles to continue the motif.

ABOVE: This eclectically furnished bathroom mixes old and new in a thoroughly modern way. Sponge-painted gold walls are enhanced by hand-painted "tassels," picked up from the gold tassels of the curtains. The wall sconce to the left of the sink has a medieval aspect. The multishelved storage unit is functional and does not obstruct the open and airy feeling created by the large, white-curtained window.

ABOVE: A rigid black–and–off-white scheme dictates this room's design. A white art deco pendant light fixture and black countertop and lacquered wood storage unit nicely tie into the theme established by the boldly striped wallpaper. Two windows surrounding a narrow mirror create symmetry in the space.

OPPOSITE: A whimsical trellis painted on the walls and cabinetry provides a unique theme in this bathroom. Artwork appears to "hang" from the painted ribbons draped over the trompe l'oeil structure and other special touches include a painted fan and basket. The mirror frames seem to be made of the same material as the trellis, completing the motif.

ABOVE: The trompe l'oeil in this bath has been done so cleverly it takes more than a glance to spot it. On closer inspection, those stately bottles and vases prove to be two-dimensional, applied with a paintbrush to their permanent perch above the dado molding. With this technique, you can have shelves of accessories without actually having to dedicate space to them—or to dust them, either!

OPTIONS IN LIGHTING

Lighting serves several purposes in the bath: it allows you to see well in order to perform a variety of tasks efficiently, it influences mood and how you feel in the space, and the fixtures themselves can be attractive decorative elements.

WHERE TO PUT LIGHT:

▨ Ideally, installing a variety of fixtures throughout the bath with separate switching and dimming options affords you a range of lighting in various areas. A portion of the room may be well lit for grooming; subdued illumination can create a romantic mood for a relaxing soak in the tub; or intense light throughout the space will permit efficient cleaning.

▨ For grooming tasks, the face should be surrounded with light. This can be achieved with a horizontal row of bulbs or fluorescent fixtures above a mirror and vertical ones down the two sides, or mount translucent fixtures at eye level to flank a mirror over the sink. Avoid placing a fixture directly overhead—this will light the top of the head beautifully, but cast shadows under the eyes, nose, and chin. Light from a fixture behind a person standing in front of a mirror will also create discomforting shadows.

▨ Tubs and showers need a good general light. Recessed fixtures with white diffusers are commonly used and quite effective. Make sure all luminaires in the shower are listed for wet locations by UL, ETL or another approved testing laboratory. There are safety regulations covering light fixtures in bath areas. For example, electrical codes state that a fixture or outlet over a whirlpool tub must be at least 7½ feet (2.3m) above the maximum water level of the tub, or at least 5 feet (1.5m) away from the closest inside wall of the tub. Exceptions are surface-mounted or recessed fixtures with glass or plastic lenses or globes and non-metallic trim that are labeled for wet locations.

TYPES OF LIGHT SOURCES:

▨ In general, incandescent bulbs produce warm tones, like red and yellow, that are flattering to the complexion. These bulbs can be dimmed easily and come on at full intensity immediately, but are the least energy-efficient and have the shortest life span.

▨ Halogen lamps produce a bright, white light that can also enhance skin tones. However, because of their intensity, care must be taken in their placement so that they do not create sharp or glaring shadow plays in large or dark-surfaced spaces. Additionally, take care to never drape anything over a halogen lamp or to place it next to flammable materials.

▨ Great strides have been made in developing fluorescent lamps that flatter complexions. Warm white, deluxe, and triphosphor lamps are fine for use in the bathroom and are energy-efficient, but avoid using cool white fluorescent. This emphasizes blues and greens in the color spectrum and gives the complexion a washed-out look. Some fluorescents take a few minutes to reach maximum intensity. Several states require fluorescents in new construction and remodeling of residential bathrooms to encourage energy-efficiency—check your local codes.

TIPS FOR CREATING GOOD QUALITY LIGHTING:

▨ Light-colored surfaces reflect more light than dark ones. Consequently, baths with very dark floors and walls will require more lighting. The more lighting fixtures you have in your bathroom, the more heat is produced; therefore make sure you have adequate ventilation to cool the room.

▨ When one passes the age of forty, the eye becomes more susceptible to glare, which is produced by the contrast between the light sources and the dark background surfaces. Older people need more illumination to see clearly what they could see at lower light levels when they were younger. A simple way to accommodate everyone is to install fixtures with higher-wattage lamps than you would normally use and include a dimmer so light levels can be adjusted easily to suit everyone's needs.

The lighting fixtures in this bathroom provide good crosslighting that illuminates both sides of the face and prevents unsightly shadows. Overhead ceiling-recessed downlights are a second lighting option that can help create a dramatic effect when needed.

✻

ABOVE: A ceiling with recessed lighting panels is decorated with painted leaves to give the bather something to look at while soaking in the tub but also draws attention to the two distinct ceiling heights in this bathroom. The stark white room is livened up by primary-colored shampoo bottles on the tub's oversize ledge. A mirror at the foot of the tub makes an interesting design statement in this deliberately stark environment.

ABOVE: Sponge-painted peach walls give this room a warm, informal glow while the green mirror achieves its antique appearance through the use of a crackle-paint finish. The tile pattern of the floor and tub surround mimic the placement of the glass block "windows," and the wood ceiling and vanity continue the warmth expressed by the palette. A skylight and the glass blocks let in natural light while maintaining privacy.

ABOVE: Sometimes simplicity is the best solution. Here, a soothing, creamy white monochromatic color scheme is enhanced by oak storage cabinets. An overhead fixture casts a soft, warm glow. A clear shower curtain gives the illusion of space while the generous marble tub ledge that matches the vanity top accommodates any bather's needs. Accessories are kept to a minimum: a bouquet of purple flowers in an aluminum pail is the room's only source of color.

ABOVE: Nature itself is the only artwork needed in this bright space. Framed by a glorious arched window, the beauty of the outdoors is reinforced by a softly painted border that is repeated around the vanity mirror. A vaulted ceiling is an unusual feature in a bathroom, and in conjunction with a floor-to-ceiling mirror on the wall opposite the vanity, serves to make the narrow space wider.

ABOVE: Striking cobalt blue painted walls and ceiling infuse this room with energy. The pristine white tub, flooring, and window frames offset the effect. An angular wood chair and traditional freestanding armoire bring warmth to the effect through the power of paint. Two large, double-paned windows let in an abundance of natural light by day. At night, the space is illuminated by bare fluorescent tubes mounted on the ceiling.

OPPOSITE: An eclectic space has been created in this bath through dark gray papered walls and ceiling and a leopard skin print carpet. Framed black-and-white photos are set against the dark gray paper creating a complementary effect. Accessories such as the red-toed slippers, sponges, books, and silver toiletries establish the personality of the decor. The mirrored wall and dado are other points of interest.

ABOVE: For a lover of pattern and ornamentation, this attic bathroom fits the bill. The tub and sink are skirted with gathered fabric and a fringed shawl is draped over the dressing table—all match the warm orange and red floor-through-ceiling wallpaper. Gilded frames around artwork—especially the ornate frame around the mirror—as well as books piled high and clutter everywhere speak of the Victorian compulsion to collect.

OPPOSITE: The storybook feel of this unusually painted orange and yellow wall creates a colorful backdrop for some equally unusual decorative pieces like the elaborately framed mirror and towel holders. The harlequin diamonds on the dado are complemented by the plaid lampshades of the decorative sconces.

✳

ABOVE: All of the interior details of this bath, especially the quaint two-legged sink, make it look like a country retreat. The delicate floral wallpaper is run onto the ceiling and the pattern is picked up again in the matching curtains. The bottom part of the wall is tiled in white to break up the effect of the bright flowers. The floral theme is repeated in the adjacent bedroom.

✳

OPPOSITE: Easy access to the outdoors is found in this compact bath. The strict patterning of the interior space with three different wallpapers contrasts the random beauty of nature in the outside garden. Wallpaper was used not only on walls, but also on the low part of the double-height ceiling and on the vanity.

CHAPTER FOUR

Materials, Surfaces, and Finishes

There is a wonderfully wide variety of materials from which to choose when installing countertops, flooring, and cabinets in your dream bath. You may consider the more typical natural stones like marble or granite, or let your imagination run wild and transform your bathroom into a study or library through the magic of wood paneling.

Granite and marble are expensive but are also durable and elegant. Granite is stronger than marble, but both are easily maintained. Bear in mind, some types of marble are more porous than others and can be easily stained by cosmetics or acidic substances. Honed stone with a matte appearance is safer than polished stone because it has more traction when wet, as do rough-cut slate, flagstone, and sandstone. Consult a professional to ensure quality and suitability of any natural stone, appropriate thickness,

and proper installation in your bath. (See Working with a Professional on page 66.)

A molded composite substance created using real marble dust bound with an unsaturated polyester resin, cultured marble is made with a corrosion-resistant polymer, and is thus stain-resistant. Cultured marble can be used for countertops, sinks, bathtubs, grab bars, and backsplashes. It can have either a matte or high-gloss finish so you have flexibility in your design if you choose this material.

Ceramic tile is another option you may consider. It is a good choice for bathrooms because it is durable, impervious to water and most liquids, easy to clean, and affordable. Grout is available in a variety of colors to complement any design scheme.

Vinyl tile and sheet vinyl are wonderful materials to use in the bathroom for a number of reasons. Vinyl is moisture-resistant and

❊

ABOVE: A wealth of natural materials has been used to beautify this bathroom. The stone tub surround is complemented by the smooth polished marble tiles of the shower walls. Rich, perfectly finished wood adorns the ceiling and sink wall. Glass block windows let in natural light while maintaining privacy.

❊

OPPOSITE: This black lacquer tub is surrounded by stone and is backed by a mirrored wall that further expands the already grand, daylight-flooded space. The soft palette of the stones underfoot is echoed by the oak wood paneling of the ceiling. Wood shutters and curtains provide privacy when windows are not being used to enjoy the mountain views. Adjustable ceiling-mounted fixtures provide light along with a wall sconce that matches the floor and tub platform.

easy to clean, and comes in a variety of colors and patterns—some vinyl is designed to look like other more elegant but higher maintenance materials like wood. And vinyl is relatively inexpensive, making it a strong choice for bathroom design.

Laminate is made of layers of resin-impregnated paper fused under pressure and bonded to particleboard or plywood. It can be used for vanity countertops, is moisture- and stain-resistant, and comes in many patterns, colors, and finishes. Generally, it is easy to clean with a damp cloth and mild cleanser, but can be damaged with caustic bathroom cleansers.

While laminate is the most popular cabinet surface for the bath, in a well-ventilated bathroom high-quality cabinets made of wood

in a natural, painted, or water-resistant washed color finish may be the best option. Although uncommon in bathroom design, wood adds a certain elegance to a bath that other materials can't achieve. But because of its reaction to water—mainly warping—it should be considered carefully. Water-resistant treatments are available to protect wood, but this material should be avoided in high-activity bathrooms. A vinyl tile that looks like wood may be your best bet.

Lastly, faux finishes give the appearance of your favorite materials, but ultimately prove to be more cost-effective and less expensive than the real thing. These finishes can be created with paint and lacquers to mimic materials like marble and stone which may appeal to you but be beyond your budget.

OPPOSITE LEFT: To relieve the darkness of the effect of the sleek charcoal tile in this bathroom while maintaining privacy, a glass block wall was installed. The simple lines of the space have been maintained in the streamlined plastic chair next to the tub and the unobtrusive towel bars.

OPPOSITE RIGHT: Luxury comes in many forms. In this bath, wood cabinets and paneling reinforce the luxuriousness created by skylights and high windows. A black, glasslike sink basin rests in a slate countertop. A large bathroom allows for lots of available storage space for toiletries and towels. Here countertop cabinets neatly conceal such eyesores as hair dryers, curling irons, and electric razors.

ABOVE: Tile is used playfully in this eclectic bath. Attention is brought to the toilet area, set up against its own bordered block of blue and red tiles, and this motif is echoed on the adjacent wall's storage area. The tables, lamp, and area rug give one side of this bath a homey look, as it if were a true extension of the other rooms of the house. The freestanding toilet paper holder adds a charming touch of brass to the decor.

ABOVE: A bath is a haven if it can transport a bather away from the cares of daily life. Here a calming space was created with lighting and texture. Rough stone gives an air of permanence and timelessness to the space while rich woods form the sink surround and countertop. Light and shadow play upon the rough surfaces of the stone through portable lamps and lighting recessed in coves around the room's perimeter.

ABOVE: The matching green lacquer sinks, toilet, bidet, and bath have rounded edges and are sleek and smooth in contrast to the rough-edged stonework in this bathroom. The windows, which echo the gridlike format of the mirrors, are frosted to allow light in from the adjacent room, while maintaining privacy for those using the bathroom. Light also enters the room through square niches backed by textured glass next to the pedestal sinks. To reinforce the feeling of symmetry, the mirror above the sinks is the same size and shape as the bathroom window. Wood paneling behind the toilet and bidet and serving as the bathtub platform introduces another texture into the room.

ABOVE LEFT: This shower and bath give the feeling of being in a cave or under a tropical waterfall. Stone in various sizes, shapes, and colors creates a mosaiclike effect in the shower and flooring for the room. The built-in stone bench in the shower provides a spot for resting. Clear glass doors easily permit light into the shower. Continuing the "natural" theme of the space is an unusual wood-paneled ceiling and a marble-topped wood vanity that offers plenty of storage opportunities, as well as display space for treasured objects.

ABOVE RIGHT: The solidity of granite in the bath makes an ideal environment from which to view the beauty of nature. A slab of polished granite acts as a tray over the bathtub for toiletries and accessories.

OPPOSITE: Muted natural tones in the towels and area rug contrast the high-tech feeling of this bath, embodied in the small greenish-gray tiles and track lighting. The two windows let in natural light, but don't take away the sense of coolness and quiet in the room. A basket at the far end of the room holds extra towels that bring a subtle dose of color to the room.

❋

ABOVE: Limestone floors and walls, along with an oversize shower enclosed by a clear glass door, make this bath seem like a desert oasis. The mahogany-framed mirrored medicine cabinet is a warm contrast to the surroundings. Sprays of white flowers, as well as all-white accessories—from hand and bath towels to bathrobes—brighten the desert palette.

ABOVE: Dense stone flooring and marble shower walls combine gracefully with a transparent shower enclosure and knotted wisps of draperies that hang next to a pristine white wall. Daylight streams into this private haven from windows set high above. The upper walls and ceiling are actually stainless steel, an interesting material for bathroom design.

❋

ABOVE: This his-and-her bath has fun with materials: the cushions of the wood storage benches are upholstered to look just like the hard granite tub surround and floor. These benches also serve as clever storage bins. The generously sized mirrors above the sinks conceal rows of shelving. Towel racks are neatly positioned beneath the sinks and adjacent to the tub.

✳

ABOVE: Granite creates a striking effect in any bath, especially in this urban space. The shelving and countertop create a perfect accent to the warmth supplied by the natural light spilling in through the vast expanse of windows. Rolled towels interspersed with decorative accessories keep the storage niches from seeming too cluttered, while maintaining their functionality.

❋

ABOVE: A raised stone bowl resting on a green smoked-glass countertop makes a striking sink. A simple faucet and spout don't detract from the beauty of the glass. Rough stone tiles give the room a rustic feel and are complemented by sleek, smooth tiles. Unusual yet functional, the placement of the mirror over the window allows walls to be used for artwork.

ABOVE: Unfinished wood paneling gives this space a rustic flair, supported further by the use of piping and valves in place of traditional faucets. Customarily, the mirror is placed directly above the sink, but because this sink is in a corner, two mirrors were installed instead. And because they have been mounted on beams that protrude out from the wood-paneled walls, they appear almost as if they are floating. Space between the beams can hold plants, towels, and toiletries. A simple white pitcher makes a delicate statement.

OPPOSITE: This bathroom evokes the feeling of "roughing it" with all the creature comforts of home. Rustic log walls are complemented by the hand-carved chair and Southwestern-style towels and pillow. A claw-foot tub and pedestal sink lend a nostalgic air. Shelving and hooks hold bath and grooming items.

ABOVE: Many rooms, especially in older houses, are not perfectly balanced, or contain structural characteristics that form variations from the typical square or rectangular room. Here, an oddly shaped room with a sloped ceiling and two atypically positioned windows is used to great advantage. The stripes of the wood panels on the walls and ceiling form a subdued backdrop to the leopard-patterned carpeting and give one the feeling of being in a ship's cabin.

ABOVE: This bath is a pine lover's dream come true. Wrought-iron hardware on the cabinetry and door handle, leather wall hangings, tools hung on the wall adjacent to the vanity, and even a mirror framed by a leather horse collar make this room a rustic retreat. A stained glass window, porcelain and brass fixtures, and the well-placed bunches of flowers add a feminine touch.

✻

ABOVE RIGHT: An abundance of wood—even in the ceiling panels—and dark tile flooring provide a lodge flavor in this unusual L-shaped bath. The antique stove and the just-built look of the vanity contribute to the bathroom's ambience. Textiles soften the space, both in the fabric and in the array of colors that contrasts with the neutral tones of the wood.

A CHILD'S BATH

Here are some tips for making a child's bath both appealing and safe:

⬚ Children are attracted to the bright and the bold, so use primary colors.

⬚ Animal motifs are fun and can take shape in wallcoverings or borders, painted or sculpted wall hangings, or inset tiles.

⬚ Rounded edges on countertops and cabinets look pleasing and can prevent injuries from a playful child's sudden movements.

⬚ Install scald guards on faucets to prevent the water from becoming hot enough to burn.

⬚ A pressure-balanced shower valve guarantees consistent water temperature and prevents sudden surges of hot water, even when a toilet is flushed.

⬚ Use strong magnetic locks on cabinet doors and drawers to keep small children away from potentially dangerous bathroom cleansers and medicines if these have to be stored in this room.

⬚ Purchase a soft bathtub with cushioned foam surrounds that prevent injuries if the child should slip.

⬚ Low-voltage lighting provides good-quality illumination and eliminates the possibility of electrical shock.

⬚ Install grab bars in and around the tub and shower.

Primary colors are appealing to children, and accent tiles in yellow, red, and blue have been scattered throughout the floor of this bath. A blazing red shower curtain and boldly patterned towels also add visual excitement to the otherwise neutral palette of the room. Fun bath toys don't need to be hidden away: a large inflatable crayon and playful sponges only add to the decor.

Animal motifs abound in this special children's bath. Twin giraffes have been placed on opposite sides of the mirror and animal portraits hang above the tub. The bathtub ledge is wide enough to hold all manner of animal toys for bathtub play. Yellow and white paint adds a cheery touch, as does the tall chair—also a great place to put towels! The "zoo" theme is completed with a small fish footstool in bold colors.

❦

ABOVE: Mosaic treatments are one of the most popular decorating techniques you can use, and are surprisingly easy to do. Here, pieces of mirror have been inlaid with cracked bits of tile to add interest. It's a playfully chaotic display confined by the contrasting, uniformly aligned whole tile squares. A series of "waves" underneath the sink completes the decoration and cleverly hides the plumbing hardware.

✳

OPPOSITE: Functional and playful with its seashore theme, this bathroom is equipped with his-and-her sinks. The oversized mirror above the vanity serves to visually "double" the space. Toiletries are cleverly tucked away in a shelving unit built into the wall.

ABOVE: Metal salamanders and seahorses act as drawer and cabinet pulls.

ABOVE, RIGHT: This mosaic critter appears throughout the space, adding a special touch of whimsy.

RIGHT: The bath's interesting mosaic tile decoration is inlaid with seashore imagery.

ABOVE: The most elaborate elements can be beautifully enhanced when surrounded by plainer details. The tiles fronting the tub and continuing up the wall behind the tub are particularly eye-catching because of the more visually "restful" surfaces that surround them: simple white walls and a geometric blue-and-white tile pattern on the vanity wall. The carved wood vanity brings the substantiality of an antique chest of drawers to this bathroom.

ABOVE: This bathroom is alive with varied textures and patterns in its surfacing materials; they give the room its unusual visual appeal. Walls paneled with vertical strips of weathered wood, the crackle-finish door, and well-weathered chair give the room a rough-hewn feel that is balanced by the cool art deco symmetry of the wall and floor tile patterns.

❊

ABOVE: Textures and materials are used nicely in this bath. Multicolored marble wall tiles and a rustic wood-framed window create an old-world flavor. Rather than conceal the plumbing pipes, this bath capitalizes on them. The glistening brass pipes and valves are complemented by the brass framework supporting the sink. Textured ceramic jars in greens and earth tones are the ideal decorative elements for this small but relaxing space.

❊

OPPOSITE: This intriguing corner is loaded with interesting materials and treatments unified through shades of one color—green. All captured in the green tile, a small three-dimensional turtle, snake, and frog add texture and variety, as does the floral motif soap dish. The painted wood mirror looks as if it was carved right out of the tile background. Brass fixtures and a brass sink basin add a brightening shock to the all-green decor.

ABOVE LEFT: The blue tiles of this bathroom give the illusion of being in a giant swimming pool. Tiles in a stepped arrangement add texture and pattern to the cool blue walls and mimic the real steps leading up to the tub.

ABOVE RIGHT: If budget permits, one interesting way to allow in sunlight while ensuring privacy is to install a stained glass window. This bathroom uses one with a contemporary interpretation.

❀

ABOVE: The diagonal tile placement in this bath creates visual interest. The green vine pattern of the border echoes the natural environment just outside the large arched windows. Lovely French doors provide a strong link between the bedroom and bath. Convenient built-in niches hold toiletries.

ABOVE: A wealth of textures comes together to create visual interest in this narrow bathroom. An unusual quilted wall treatment contrasts with a smooth tile border, and then moves into a rough faux stone wall treatment. The medicine cabinet, shelving, and towel bars are functional and simple, so as not to distract from the other, more important design elements.

❋

ABOVE: This bathroom is made luxurious through the use of creamy marble and rich wood. The top portions of the vanity cabinets appear to be only a trim but are really handleless drawers; the lower portions contain open compartments ideal for storage of towels. Wide traffic areas and large square windows create the illusion of space.

❋

ABOVE: Though the surface materials change from the bedroom to the bath in this elegant example, the palette remains the same. The rough-textured stone of the bathtub surround is a good contrast to the smooth-tiled floor. Simply including a place to be seated can make the space more functional and enjoyable.

✳

ABOVE: Just when you think sleek and smooth is the whole story in this bathroom—the bull-nosed countertop, the glistening drawer pulls, and rounded vanity—the rough mortar and brick wall adds another dimension. Textured wallpaper that looks like unfinished wood (shown in the mirror over the vanity) also adds to the effect. Natural and electric light are provided by double windows and wall-mounted sconces, respectively.

ABOVE: Here, colors and materials are mixed and matched. Different hues of gray come across in the pearlized hand-printed wallpaper complemented by a moire finish on doors and door frames. A beautifully detailed wood built-in storage unit holds clothes and accessories. The use of metal in objets d'art and glass-fronted closet doors add to the openness and contemporary ambience of the space.

❋

ABOVE: A vertical row of windows with a curvy bench creates a wonderful divider to a pair of classical column porcelain pedestal sinks. The seating is unobtrusive and multifunctional—for sitting or for resting towels. Wide ledges around the sinks are perfect for keeping toiletries.

CHAPTER FIVE

Fixtures and Accessories

The variety of fixtures and fittings available today will allow you to completely personalize your bathroom decor—down to the smallest detail. It's important to understand what your options are before you embark on installing or replacing your bathroom fixtures.

There are two main types of sinks available: countertop or vanity sinks and pedestal sinks. Countertop sinks can be mounted in four ways: self-rimming sinks sit atop the countertop cutout; integral basins are part of the countertop itself; tile-in sinks are installed flush with a tile counter; and undermounted sinks are installed from underneath the counter. Pedestal sinks, on the other hand, are freestanding with the plumbing pipes concealed by a decorative base.

Sink basins may be round or rectangular shaped, or can, in some cases, be creatively shaped. Custom colors and hand-painted designs

or gold trims may adorn sink basins. Faucets can be sleek and modern, antique-style, or whimsical in nature—there is something available to please every personality.

For the most part, bathtubs are made from enameled steel, gel-coat fiberglass-reinforced polyester, cast iron, acrylic, or cultured marble. The standard tub is 5 feet (1.5m) long and about 14 inches (35cm) deep. Prices go up the larger and more equipped the tub: custom colors, unusual materials, and comfort features such as lumbar support, built-in grab bars, or slip-resistant bottoms will affect the cost.

Either as a separate unit or built in conjunction with the bathtub, the shower can be made into a luxurious spa with body sprays, dual showerheads, or seats for shaving or relaxing. In some cases, you can combine your showerhead with a steam generator that converts your shower into a relaxing steam bath. Standard showers are 32 or 36 inches (81 or 91cm) square.

ABOVE: Any bath has room for a touch of whimsy. Here, the hot and cold water controls are in the shapes of a cute little bird and rabbit.

OPPOSITE: A striking look is created by this shimmering oyster shell sink mounted on a marble countertop. The faucet and spout that project out from the mirror set a dramatic mood. Fresh flowers are always welcome additions in brightening and beautifying a space.

Probably the most cost-effective way you can update the decor of your shower is choosing fittings—faucets, spouts, showerheads, and other types of water-carrying and water-controlling hardware.

Waterfall or flume spouts and gold-plated handles are just some of the attractive hardware options. Look for faceted, textured, or levered handles and knobs—they will be the easiest to turn when wet.

Showerheads can be wall- or ceiling-mounted, or can be detachable. A handheld showerhead is great for bathing children and pets, and cleaning the shower area. Adjustable spray jets can be mounted on one wall or opposite walls of the shower to provide hydro massage and full-body showers. Also available are rain bars that can be installed on your shower walls or ceiling. These have as many as twenty openings in a single bar, creating a fine mist of water.

The standard height of a toilet bowl is 15 inches (38cm). Most toilets are made of glazed vitreous china. Standard models are equipped with two parts—a tank and a round or elongated bowl—but more expensive one-piece models are also available.

More common in Europe than in the United States, the bidet is more expensive than the toilet. Low-end bidets have basin-mounted faucets; the most expensive have water running through the rim. The bidet is usually selected to match the color and style of the toilet and installed along the same wall. Other luxury items such as electric floor-warming systems; wall, under-the-sink, and overhead heaters; towel warmers; miniwashers and dryers; and whirlpools, steam baths, and saunas may also be part of your plan.

If your budget stands in the way of installing luxury fixtures that truly personalize your bath, don't forget about accessories. Simple finishing touches like soap dishes, toothbrush holders, trays for toiletries, and vases bursting with blooming flowers are all economical ways to spruce up your bath and make it your own.

ABOVE: Faucet styles abound in the marketplace today, many with features that allow for easier installation and offer more options than in the past. Even if you have a bathtub separate from the shower, it can be a welcome convenience to include a handheld showerhead for use in the tub for washing objects too large to handle in the sink and pets.

OPPOSITE: A bowl-shaped sink carved from granite—smooth on the inside, but roughly textured on the outside—is cleverly set on a classical column, giving the space the feel of antiquity. Dragonfly faucets perched over the edge add a whimsical touch. Below the mirrored walls a border of stonework completes the design.

✾

OPPOSITE: A thin granite counter supported by metal legs is a focal point in this sleek and modern bath. The mirror seems to float in space, but is actually supported by strong, thin wires. White tiles enhance the minimalist style and concrete-textured flooring adds to the tactile appeal of the space. Compartmentalized storage bins rest in tubular metal frames below the countertop. The atypical sinks are two different sizes to accommodate various needs.

✾

ABOVE LEFT: Combining the unexpected can create particular interest in a bath. A glass sink bowl is set into an opaque metal counter. The walls and backsplash are made with yet another element—marble tile. The curved towel rack below the sink matches the slim, curving metal faucet handles and spout.

✾

ABOVE RIGHT: One way to make the most of a small space is to position the sink in the corner, and place the mirror to the right or to the left. The corners of the triangle countertop surrounding this sink provide enough resting places for toiletries and decorative accessories, such as a vase of fresh tulips that infuses the space with color. And just because a bathroom is small doesn't mean it can't be elegant as evidenced in the glistening hammered steel bowl.

❋

ABOVE: This stainless steel sink and countertop are formed from one sheet to create a streamlined look. The all-in-one faucets and spouts contribute to the clean lines of the vanity. Warming up the cold metal are wood elements—the two chairs and the framework encasing the mirror and light fixtures. This high-volume space also has cubbyholes near the ceiling that can be used for long-term storage or display.

ABOVE: Variations in height and depth provide an abundance of visually interesting storage solutions that allow this bathroom to look uncluttered. Mirrored cabinets are "broken up" and made more appealing by changing the length and including a small niche at one end. Cabinets below the countertops are varied in height and depth and line two walls of the bath. Exposed shelves above the sink and next to one side of the window hold frequently used toiletries and towels. The uncluttered look is continued through streamlined fittings in the wall, rather than in the countertop above the sink. Simple cabinet pulls and towel bars complete the picture.

ABOVE LEFT: Two white, simply shaped sinks on either side of a vertical wooden storage unit make for a modern look and provide visual interest. The storage unit is well-equipped with a multitude of drawers to hold everything from cosmetics to hair products. Daylight streams in at varied heights from three small stacked windows.

ABOVE RIGHT: The owner of this bath has no trouble catching the morning or late-night news with a small television positioned safely and securely adjacent to the tub, an accessory that would be welcome in any bath. Chrome and glass accessories provide just the right ornamentation in this pristine room.

OPPOSITE: Mirrors can be used creatively to spice up your decor. Here, gold frames and a circular mirror hung in front of an already mirrored wall create a wonderful effect. The vanity cabinetry is carved from rich wood and the countertop, floor, and bathtub surround are in complementary shades of green.

OPPOSITE: Repetition is used to create interest as well as a sense of unity in this bath. The shape of the high square windows is repeated in the white tile walls and bathtub surround featuring black inset tiles. The rounded pedestal sinks break up the geometric effect.

ABOVE LEFT: This bath has been transformed from an ordinary room into a unique retreat rich with character. A great way to take advantage of a high ceiling in the bath is to line the upper portion of the walls with shelves for objets d'art and other personal mementos.

ABOVE RIGHT: Sometimes it is possible to expand a small bath in an older home by using an adjacent corridor to enlarge the space, or to accommodate some of the grooming functions. Here, the sink is set in a marble countertop with marble backsplash and side panels. The antique wooden chair toilet graces the space with old-fashioned charm.

OPPOSITE: On a cold winter's night, a languorous bath by a roaring fire can be a relaxing reprieve. A bathroom doesn't have to be large or elaborate to fulfill your dreams of comfort and relaxation. Personally chosen details such as the wicker chairs and the painted frame mirror can make any space special.

ABOVE LEFT: This attic bathroom is filled with playful fixtures and accessories. A Victorian sink resides under a wood-framed mirror that is adorned on either side by "tulip" sconces. A shelving unit provides the perfect place to put pictures and personal objects, and an assortment of toiletries. The window has been painted over to provide privacy while at the same time allowing light in.

ABOVE RIGHT: The right accessories have made this interestingly tiled corner with an extraordinary clawfoot tub a romantic spot to unwind. An upholstered chair on the right is a comfortable place to wait for water to fill the tub. A straw basket holds towels in a more decorative way than hooks or shelves. The vase of fresh flowers adds a special delicate touch.

ABOVE LEFT: Simplicity can make a small space very efficient. Here, an open shower is separated from the vanity by a vertical glass partition. A flexible handheld showerhead helps the bather keep the water flow under control.

ABOVE RIGHT: This master bath shower is equipped with speakers that pipe in music during shower time. For convenience, there are two showerheads: one wall-mounted and the other handheld.

OPPOSITE: Sleek and modern, this his-and-her bath is filled with fine details. Two vertical lighting units fit snugly on either side of the arched mirrors. Matching shelves beneath the mirrors have metal water beakers and a pair of light switches and outlets on either side. A thick aluminum pole serves as a towel rack below the sinks, and a simple stripe and square pattern adorns the perimeter of the room (as seen in the mirrors).

ABOVE LEFT: This custom-designed showerhead in a high-ceilinged pool house provides a pleasurable shower. Its vast number of pinhole openings have a rainlike effect.

ABOVE RIGHT: Toiletries can be stored in style in matching containers on a tray in your bath. If you don't have a matching set of containers and jars for your bath—no problem. These transparent jars have pretty silver tops, yet it's easy to see at a glance what's in them and when they are due for refilling. Instead of leaving one lone bar of soap near the sink, try placing several in various scents and colors in a bowl—they look lush and are at hand when a replacement is needed.

LEFT: Decorative bottles and vases as well as toiletries are cleverly stored in this paneled bathroom on shelves that cover the perimeter of the room, as reflected in the mirror.

EXTENDING THE COMFORT ZONE

Many people consider the bath to be more than just a functional room. This concept of a bathroom as a place to relax and eradicate the stress of the workday has led to expanding its uses to encompass other activities, as well as extending it into other areas of the home. Here are some options for creating a bath that is more than a bath:

※ The showering required after a good workout has prompted some to include exercise equipment in the bath, or in a room adjacent to it. Keep in mind that exercise equipment should be positioned on nonskid surfaces with enough space allowed around the equipment for comfortable movement of arms and legs during exercising. And how about installing a miniwasher and dryer for easy laundering of gym clothes?

※ The blending of indoor and outdoor activities in warmer climates has led to positioning an indoor bath near the outdoor pool or hot tub.

※ A merging of outside and inside also occurs when window walls allow views into private gardens beyond. Plants and foliage with ample daylight from windows and skylights bring a refreshing spa quality to the bath, while saunas and steam baths create a tropical paradise of comfort in the home.

※ Place a whirlpool or hot tub in a sunroom or miniconservatory filled with plants and furnished with comfortable upholstered chairs and sofas to bring the feeling of nature and the outdoors inside the home.

※ Include an entertainment center, equipped with a tape or CD player for listening to music or books on tape, and a radio or small television to get traffic and weather reports and the news of the morning.

※ The bathroom can be a place where a couple can be together and unwind at the end of the day. Besides a tub, whirlpool, hot tub, and shower built for two, a large bathroom can include a warming fireplace and oversized comfy pillows scattered before it. A minirefrigerator and bar area nearby can hold wine, mineral water, or other special treats.

※ Master baths have also become extensions of the bedroom, with the lines blurred between sitting rooms, dressing rooms, and the bath. The style in which the bedroom is decorated can be extended to the bath to make the suite more of a visually unified whole.

Even if you don't have a large bath, there are touches of luxury you can include to make the space you do have special:
• Towel-warming bars
• Gold-plated faucets
• Warming units installed under floor tiles
• Multispeed showerheads

ABOVE: The occupant of this space can soak in a sumptuous whirlpool and keep in shape by exercise any time of the year. Glass everywhere in the sloped ceiling panels and windows is great for enjoying the beautiful view and for keeping the not-so-nice natural elements out on cold and dreary days.

ABOVE: For some, the bath is far more than a functional place. It is a private retreat to get away from household chaos and catch up on reading. Here, a tub tray cradles the latest bestseller. An imitation Eileen Gray side table is at hand to hold a favorite beverage or snack. Artwork is placed at bathing level for easy viewing in moments of reverie.

OPPOSITE: One advantage of a large bathroom is the ability to include separate shower and tub spaces. Here, the shower is fitted with two shower bars that yield comforting water sprays, whether you're standing or sitting—the shower space is ample enough to include a portable chair. Lighting is provided by large windows during the day and a waterproof lighting fixture at night. The cream-colored tiling makes the brass sink and surrounding black and gold countertop stand out and nicely complements the patio area and garden outside.

ABOVE LEFT: This bath takes an unusual approach to design with a light installed in the shower floor, a shower surrounded by clear glass panels, and the interesting metal circular sink and its piping. The contrasting brass piping that frames the mirror above the sink and the dangling tubing of the handheld showerhead also add to this outrageous design. The toilet is minimal—with an unobtrusive tank and sans cover. White tile walls surround and highlight this minimalist bath in which the clustered fixtures and fittings that provide the central functions in the room are appropriately placed in the center of the room.

ABOVE RIGHT: His-and-her vanities can be treated as "separate but equal," or they can share certain elements, as is the case in this bath. A clean look comes from the use of mirrored wall, the continuous light fixture above and ledge below. There's also plenty of space on the countertop for each of the users, even though it is shared.

OPPOSITE: Sometimes a large space can offer the opportunity to create a room that looks very unlike a bathroom. Here, a frosted glass compartment houses the toilet. Beyond this, toward the sliding glass doors, a similar clear glass compartment encloses the shower area. Plain and simple open racks hold towels.

ABOVE: The cool mystery of dark marble tile in this shower area is enhanced by the interplay of light and shadow. General illumination comes from ceiling-recessed fixtures; additional light comes through the window. The clear glass shower enclosure allows the space to seem large and open. The shower wall niche is ideal for holding plants and toiletries.

ABOVE: This deep freestanding metal tub, semicircular towel bar, and angled window help create a space-age ambience in this narrow bathroom.
The stepped partition with glass-block risers adds to the techno feel.

ABOVE: A combination of elements makes this bath dramatic. Mosaic tile, stainless steel, and marble combine to transport the bather to another world. The draped fabric shower curtain adds elegance. A glass block wall provides both light and privacy, and is a stark contrast to harder materials.

❈

ABOVE: This minimalist bath has a spalike feeling with its glass block wall, white tiles, contrasting black flooring, and the unusual freestanding showerhead and stem.

ABOVE: An unusual fixture, this freestanding vanity and mirror serves as a divider in a large bathroom that is decorated with wood and stone. The polished wood is a sophisticated contrast to the rough stone flooring.

OPPOSITE: A wood cylinder encases this sink with easy-to-operate lever handles and a gooseneck faucet. The sheer shower curtain adds a feminine touch to the bath. Two glass vases containing single flowers provide just enough decoration in the sparse space.

ABOVE: The vanity counter of this bathroom makes the space especially appealing. With no drawers beneath a countertop, it offers a comfortable spot to sit. The storage unit adjacent to the countertop is a pleasing combination of exposed shelving where photos and decorative items can be displayed. A handy shelf sits between the generously sized pedestal sink and its ornate mirror.

ABOVE: A fantasy bath can easily be achieved in a small space. To evoke the feeling of early twentieth-century Paris, this freestanding corner tub has been surrounded with yards of gauzy curtains, a comfortable chair, a romantic window seat, and a wooden bath tray to hold some comforting accessories.

ABOVE: An interesting way to provide a divider between the toilet area and the rest of the bath, this stained glass partition is custom-made and held in a wooden arched frame suspended by a lovely decorative armature.

OPPOSITE: The old-fashioned pull-chain toilet tank mounted in the corner of this bathroom gives it a firmly Victorian identity. A stained glass window, an ornate lighting fixture, and a gold-framed mirror all serve to evoke the ambience of a bygone era.

ABOVE: Custom-designed cabinetry extends the comfort zone of any bath. Here, ribbed glass conceals an abundance of bath items—towels, soaps, sponges, cleansers, and toiletries. Small drawers at the top are ideal for holding accessories. Basic black fixtures blend into the background and don't compete with the natural wood beauty of the cabinet.

ABOVE: What better bathroom could there be for the avid reader? A small table holds a candle and a short-armed sconce is mounted near the window—and there are books everywhere. Most are real, except for some faux spines on the wall below the window. The design even includes a wooden library ladder.

What's New from the National Kitchen and Bath Association?

NATIONAL KITCHEN & BATH ASSOCIATION SURVEY

WHAT SELLS IN BATHS

How do your preferences stack up against what Certified Bathroom Designers reported when surveyed in 1996 by the National Kitchen & Bath Association (NKBA)? The following are the highlights of that survey:

- The average price for a bath is $9,000, according to those surveyed. That price reflects a complete job, including new cabinets, counters, fixtures, flooring, and the labor required for tear-out and installation.

- Cabinetry accounts for a majority percentage of this total investment. Designers report that more than half of the cabinets being sold are custom-designed and made. Semicustom cabinets are also popular. Less than a quarter of the cabinets being sold are stock.

- Bathrooms are becoming specialized spaces. The designers reported that more than half of the bathroom jobs being completed are master suites. Guest rooms, powder rooms, and bathrooms designed specifically for children are also popular.

- Whirlpools are incorporated in 39 percent of bathroom renovations; make-up/grooming centers in 35 percent; and stereo/television centers in 11 percent. About 48 percent of bathroom projects include a separate tub and shower, and 49 percent include more than one lavatory.

- Solid surface countertops are incorporated in 39 percent of bathrooms, while 28 percent include cultured marble, and 21 percent are laminate. But the use of granite and tile is increasing. Certified Bathroom Designers indicated that tile and granite are each used in 9 percent of bathroom renovation projects.

KITCHEN & BATH PLANNING KIT

A Remodeling Planning Kit for consumers is available from the National Kitchen and Bath Association (NKBA). This kit includes the following:

- *The Little Book of Kitchen and Bath Wisdom* which provides basic information on the steps to take and what to expect when embarking on a kitchen or bath renovation project.

- A quadrille pad for sketching and note taking.

- Referrals to NKBA members, including kitchen/bath dealers, Certified Kitchen/Bathroom Designers, multibranch retail firms, and decorative plumbing and hardware showrooms.

- A list of manufacturers' addresses/phone numbers to assist you in gathering information.

- A folder that can be used to keep all the information about your bathroom project in one place.

Consumers can purchase the NKBA's remodeling kit for a nominal fee by calling the NKBA at (800) 401-NKBA, ext. 710, or by writing to NKBA at Box 2375, Chatsworth, California 91313.

THE NATIONAL KITCHEN & BATH ASSOCIATION (NKBA)

The 6,000-member NKBA is a trade association representing all segments of the kitchen and bathroom industry. It provides education, certification, consumer awareness, business management, and legislative awareness services for kitchen and bath design professionals as well as for consumers.

Sources

page 2
Design 1/Marilee Schemp
Summit, NJ
(908) 277-1110

pages 7, 11
Yvette Gervey
Boca Raton, FL
(407) 392-3726

pages 8 top, 49, 79
SGH Designs
New York, NY
(212) 421-1950

pages 8 bottom, 69, 138, 142, 147, 158, 159
Brian Murphy
Santa Monica, CA
(310) 459-0955

pages 9, 20, 108
John Saladino
New York, NY
(212) 752-2440

page 14
J. Rolf Seckinger, Inc.
Miami, FL
(305) 673-1566

page 17
Stemberg & Aferiat Architecture
New York, NY
(212) 255-4173

pages 18, 51, 63
Samuel Botero Associates
New York, NY
(212) 935-5155

page 19
Boxwood House/ Melinda Johnson
Tenafly, NJ
(201) 871-3323

page 21
Sally Bennett
New York, NY
(212) 750-3995

page 23
Janice McCarthy
Los Angeles, CA
(213) 651-4229

pages 31, 118, 126
Madeline Stuart
Los Angeles, CA
(213) 935-3305

page 32 left
Joe Terrell
Los Angeles, CA
(213) 469-8044

page 35
Daly-Genik
Los Angeles, CA
(310) 656-3180

pages 36, 47
Charlotte Moss & Co.
New York, NY
(212) 772-6244

pages 40, 67, 110 left
Michael Berman Design
Los Angeles, CA
(213) 655-9813

pages 43, 64
Lembo-Bohn Design Associates, Inc.
New York, NY
(212) 645-3636

page 53
Jennie Curland
Stuart, FL
(407) 287-1696

pages 55, 78, 123
Inez Foose
New York, NY
(718) 486-5692

page 60 right
Centerbrook Architects
Centerbrook, CT
(860) 767-0175

page 68
Rios Associates, Inc.
Los Angeles, CA
(213) 852-6717

pages 70, 81
Bonnie Siracusa
Great Neck, NY
(516) 482-3349

page 72
Francis Mah
Memphis, TN
(901) 754-8721

pages 74, 83
Sleepscot Stenciling
Alna, ME
(207) 586-5692

page 76
Kerry Joyce
Los Angeles, CA
(213) 938-4442

page 77
Michael de Santis, Inc.
New York, NY
(212) 753-8871

page 82
Hutchings-Lyle
New York, NY
(212) 288-2729

page 88
Wirth-Salander Studios Georgette and Kim
South Norwalk, CT
(203) 852-9449

page 91
David Barrett, FASID
New York, NY
(212) 688-0950

page 92
Norman Michaeloff
New York, NY
(212) 288-5400

page 93
Derrick & Love
New York, NY
(212) 777-3113

page 94
Robert Segal Architecture
New York, NY
(212) 366-9425

page 97
Paul Erdman, Architect
Oyster Bay, NY
(516) 922-7962

page 100
Thread Needle Street of Montclair/Janet Blanchard

pages 102, 111
Doris La Porte
New York, NY
(212) 874-0716

page 103
Joe Ruggiero
Encino, CA
(818) 783-9256

page 104
Stephenson's Construction
Attleborough, MA
(508) 222-8198

pages 109, 168
Richard Rawson/Richard's Kitchen and Bath Center
Upper Montclair, NJ
(201) 783-1336

page 112,144
Smith & Thompson
New York, NY
(212) 865-0151

page 115
Hoffman, Vest & Associates
Santa Monica, CA
(310) 828-8010

page 117
Chris Campbell Gorman Richardson Architects
Hopkinton, MA
(508) 497-2590

page 120
JoAnne M. Kuehner
Naples, FL
(813) 434-6001

page 122 right
Ann Fitzpatrick Brown
Stockbridge, MA
(413) 298-5565

pages 124, 125
Dwight Gregory
Santa Barbara, CA
(805) 682-8760

page 127
Freehand
New York, NY

pages 128, 130 right
Chris Hill
San Antonio, TX

page 129
Country Floors
New York, NY
(212) 627-8300

page 131
Laura Baker
Los Angeles, CA
(310) 573-1232

page 132
Mark Zeff Consulting Group, Inc.
New York, NY
(212) 580-7090

page 135
Stephen Ackerman Designs
New York, NY
(212) 633-1900

page 141
Nicholas Calder Interiors
New York, NY
(212) 861-9055

pages 143, 146
Mojo Stumer
Roslyn, NY
(516) 625-3344

page 145
Haverson Architecture and Design
New York, NY
(212) 889-4182

page 148
Steven Erhlich, Architect
Venice, CA
(310) 399-7711

page 151
K-Design
Port Washington, NY
(516) 944-9796

page 152 left
Four Seasons Green Houses
Holbrook, NY
(516) 563-4000

page 152 right
John B. Schollz
Camden, ME
(207) 236-0777

page 153
Peter Carlson
Los Angeles, CA
(213) 969-8423

page 154 top left
Perry Dean Rogers & Partners
Boston, MA
(617) 423-0100

page 154 bottom left
Max King
Calistoga, CA

page 160
Pei Partnership
New York, NY
(212) 674-9000

page 166
Vogel and Mulea Designs
Lawrence, NY
(516) 239-3503

page 170
Neil Korpinen
Los Angeles, CA
(213) 661-9861

Index

Photo Credits

©Philip Beaurline: pp. 32 right, 45, 57, 105

©M. Grazia Branco: pp. 8 middle, 25, 38, 48, 85, 98, 130 left

©Grey Crawford: pp. 32 left (Designer: Joe Terrell), 67 (Designer: Michael Berman), 68 (Designer: Rio, Architect), 96 (Designer: Charles Ward), 110 left (Designer: Michael Berman), 115 (Designer: Ellen Hoffman & Associates), 148 (Designer: Steven Erhlich Architecture), 157

©Derrick & Love: pp. 82 both (Designer: Hutchings-Lyle), 93 (Designer: Derrick and Love)

©Philip Ennis: pp. 2 (Designer: Design I/Marilee Schemp), 8 top (Designer: SGH Designs), 18 (Designer: Sameul Botero Associates), 19 (Designer: Boxwood House/Melinda Johnson), 27 (Designer: Blodgett/ Hatley Designs), 49 (Designers: SGH Designs), 51 (Designer: Sameul Botero Associates), 77 (Designer: Michael de Santis, Inc.), 79 (Designer: SGH Designs), 97 (Designer: Paul Erdman, Architect), 129 (Designer: Country Floors), 135 (Designer: Stephen Ackerman Designs), 141 (Designer: Nicholas Calder Interiors), 143 left (Designer: Mojo-Simmer, Architect), 146 right (Designer: Mojo-Simmer, Architect), 151 both (Designer: K-Design), 152 left, 155 (Designer: Four Seasons Green Houses), 171 (Designer: Kemp-Simmers)

Esto: ©Peter Aaron: pp. 163, 165; ©Otto Baitz: p. 80; ©Mark Darley: pp. 106 right, 143 right, 158 right; ©Scott Francis: pp. 28 both, 162; ©Norman McGrath: pp. 12, 73 left, 106 left, 122 left

©Feliciano: pp. 13 (Home of Eileen Dahl and Mark Rosen), 107 (Designer: Howard Graff)

©Tria Giovan: pp. 154 top right, 167

©Green World Pictures/Mick Hales: pp. 137, 139, 150, 156, 169

©Steve Gross and Susan Daley: pp. 10, 33, 44 (Designer: Steve Bernstein, NYC), 55, 78, 123 (Designer: Inez Foose, NYC), 127 (Designer: Freehand, NYC), 128, 130 right (Designer: Chris Hill, San Antonio)

©image/dennis krukowski: pp. 6 top, 6 middle (Designer: Tom O' Toole, Inc.), 14 (Designer: Rolf J. Seckinger), 21 (Designer: Sally Bennett), 29 (Designer: Brenda Speight), 36, 47 (Designer: Charlotte Moss & Co.), 52 (Designer: Tom O'Toole, Inc.), 63 (Designer: Sam Botero Associates), 87 (Designer: H.A. Fields Design Studios), 88 (Designer: Wirth-Salander Studios), 99 (Designer Ned Marshall, Inc.), 100 (Designer: Thread Needle Street of Montclair/Janet Blanchard), 101 (Designer: David Solomon), 119, (Designer: Suzie Frankfort), 120 (Designer: Jo Anne Koehner), 121 (Designer: Loey Ringquist), 122 right (Designer: Ann Fitzpatrick Brown), 132 (Designer: Mark Zeff Consulting Group),

136 (Designer: Atelier/Christine Lambert), 149 left (Designer: Robert B. Greene III Decoration), 149 right (Hearst Ranch/Piedra Blanca Rancho)

©Nancy Hill: p. 37 (Designer: Stephen Gilden, Inc.)

Courtesy of Kohler Company: pp. 109, 168 (Designer: Richard Rawson/Richard's Kitchen and Bath Center)

©David Livingston: pp. 23 left, 24, 39, 41 both, 46, 56, 58, 59, 60 left, 61, 62, 65, 71, 73 right, 89, 95, 114, 133, 140

©Michael Mundy: pp. 153 (Architect: Dreamer and Phillips; Designer: Peter Carlson), 161 (Architect/Designer: Michael Kalil)

©David Phelps: pp. 16, 50, 86 (Designer: Dana Van Kleeck; Decorative painting: Karen Linder), 124 (Architect: Dwight Gregory, Santa Barbara, Courtesy *American Homestyle & Gardening*), 125 all three (Architect: Dwight Gregory, Santa Barbara, Courtesy *American Homestyle & Gardening*), 154 bottom left (Designer: Max King, Calistoga , CA)

©Eric Roth: pp. 26, 104 (Designer: Stephenson's Construction)

©Bill Rothschild: pp. 7, 11 (Designer: Yvette Gervey), 53 (Designer: Jennie Curland), 70, 81 (Designer: Bonnie Siracusa), 84 (Designers: Benincasa & Gowan), 91 (Designer: David Barrett, F.A.S.I.D.),

92 (Designer: Norman Michaeloff), 166 (Designers: Celia Vogel & Mario Mulea)

©Tim Street-Porter: pp. 8 bottom (Designer: Brian Murphy), 15 (Designer: Frank Dennino; Walls painted by Christian Granuelle), 42 (Designer: Russ Leiland), 69 (Designer: Brian Murphy), 75 (Designer: Richard Rouillard), 103 (Designer: Joe Ruggiero), 110 right (Designer: Russ Leiland), 116 (Designer: Leslie Harris), 138 (Designer: Brian Murphy), 142 (Designer: Brian Murphy), 146 left (Designer: Jeffrey Tohl), 147 (Designer: Brian Murphy), 158 left (Designer: Brian Murphy), 159 (Designer: Brian Murphy), 170 (Designer: Neil Korpinen)

©Brian Vanden Brink: pp. 30, 54 (Architects: Sargent, Webster, Crenshaw & Folley), 60 right (Centerbrook Architects), 74, 83 (Stenciling: Sheepscot Stenciling), 102, 111 (Designer: Doris La Porte), 117 (Architect: Chris Campbell), 152 right (Architect: John B. Schollz), 154 top left (Architects: Perry Dean Rogers & Partners)

©Dominique Vorillon: pp. 9, 20 (Designer: John Saladino), 22 (Designer: Amy Pascal), 23 right(Designer: Janice McCarthy), 31 34 (Designer: Madeline Stuart), 35 (Designer: Daly-Genik), 40 (Designer: Michael Berman), 43, 64 (Designer: Lembo-Bohn), 76 (Designer: Kerry Joyce), 90 (Designer: Deborah Stroloff), 108 (Designer: John Saladino), 113 (Designer: Belson),

118, 126 (Designer: Madeline Stuart), 131 (Designer: Laura Balzer), 134, 164 right (Designer: Belson)

©Paul Warchol: pp. 17 (Designer: Stamberg & Aferiat Architecture), 72 (Designer: Nancy Mah), 94 (Designer: Robert Segal Architecture), 112, 144 (Designer: Smith & Thompson), 145 (Designer: Haverson Architecture and Design), 160 (Designer: Pei Partnership)

LIFE

100
Photographs
THAT CHANGED
THE WORLD

LIFE

100 Photographs

THAT CHANGED
THE WORLD

LIFE

100
Photographs
THAT CHANGED
THE WORLD

LIFE

Managing Editor Robert Sullivan
Creative Director Ian Denning
Picture Editor Barbara Baker Burrows
Executive Editor Robert Andreas
Deputy Picture Editor Christina Lieberman
Senior Reporter Hildegard Anderson
Writer-Reporter Carol Vinzant
Copy JC Choi (Chief), Mimi McGrath, Wendy Williams
Production Manager Michael Roseman
Picture Research Lauren Steel
Photo Assistant Joshua Colow
Consulting Picture Editors
Suzanne Hodgart (London), Tala Skari (Paris)

Editorial Operations Richard K. Prue (Director), Brian Fellows (Manager),
Keith Aurelio, Charlotte Coco, Tracey Eure, Kevin Hart, Mert Kerimoglu,
Rosalie Khan, Patricia Koh, Marco Lau, Brian Mai, Po Fung Ng,
Rudy Papiri, Robert Pizaro, Barry Pribula, Clara Renauro, Katy Saunders,
Vaune Trachtman

Time Home Entertainment

Publisher Richard Fraiman
General Manager Steven Sandonato
Executive Director, Marketing Services Carol Pittard
Executive Director, Retail & Special Sales Tom Mifsud
Executive Director, New Product Development Peter Harper
Director, Bookazine Development & Marketing Laura Adam
Publishing Director Joy Butts
Assistant General Counsel Helen Wan
Book Production Manager Suzanne Janso
Design & Prepress Manager Anne-Michelle Gallero
Brand Manager Roshni Patel

Special thanks to Christine Austin, Jeremy Biloon, Glenn Buonocore,
Malati Chavali, Jim Childs, Susan Chodakiewicz, Rose Cirrincione,
Jacqueline Fitzgerald, Carrie Frazier Hertan, Christine Font, Lauren Hall,
Malena Jones, Mona Li, Robert Marasco, Kimberly Marshall, Amy
Migliaccio, Nina Mistry, Dave Rozzelle, Ilene Schreider, Adriana Tierno,
Alex Voznesenskiy, Jonathan White, Vanessa Wu

Published by

LIFE Books

an imprint of Time Home
Entertainment Inc.
135 West 50th Street,
New York, NY 10020

ISBN 10: 1-60320-176-9

ISBN 13: 978-1-60320-176-6

Library of Congress Control
Number: 2011922064

Iconic images from the LIFE Picture Collection are now available
as fine art prints and posters. The prints are reproductions
on archival, resin-coated photographic paper, framed in black
wood, with an acid-free mat. Works by the famous LIFE
photographers—Eisenstaedt, Parks, Bourke-White, Burrows,
among many others—are available. The LIFE poster collection
presents large-format, affordable, suitable-for-framing images.
For more information on the prints, priced at $99 each, call
888-933-8873 or go to www.purchaseprints.com. The posters
may be viewed and ordered at www.LIFEposters.com.

We welcome your comments
and suggestions about LIFE
Books. Please write to us at:
LIFE Books, Attention:
Book Editors, PO Box 11016,
Des Moines, IA 50336-1016

If you would like to order any
of our hardcover Collector's
Edition books, please call us
at 1-800-327-6388 (Monday
through Friday, 7:00 a.m.–
8:00 p.m. or Saturday, 7:00
a.m.–6:00 p.m. Central Time).

Please visit us, and
sample past editions of
LIFE, at www.LIFE.com.

The Premise Behind These Pictures

Let us first pose a question: Is it folly to nominate 100 photographs as having been influential to world events, or is this a valid historic inquiry? LIFE will, here and in the following pages, put forth its argument. You be the judge.

Having been in the business of presenting stirring, revelatory photography since 1936, LIFE has a vested interest in claiming for photojournalism a place of high importance. Given its preferences and an endless page count, LIFE would put forth a thousand and more photos of substance, each of them worth at least a thousand words.

Words. Ever since chisel was taken to stone, it has been accepted that words can and do change the world. Whether it be the Torah, the New Testament or the Koran, the Magna Carta or the Declaration of Independence, *J'Accuse, Oliver Twist* or *Catch-22, Common Sense* or *Silent Spring,* the effect of words can reach so many hearts and minds that it impacts the human condition and the course of mankind. Speeches incite, editorials persuade, poems inspire.

Can photographs perform similarly?

For several weeks in the spring of 2003, LIFE solicited answers to that question on its own Web site (www.LIFE.com) and that of the highly regarded *Digital Journalist* (www.digitaljournalist.org), an online publication affiliated with the University of Texas. We received many opinions, most of which supported our conceit that a photo could change the world—music to our ears—along with one detailed, intelligent rebuttal. "I really do not believe that photographs actually change anything, least of all the 'World,'" wrote Joshua Haruni. "To suggest that photographs, like the written word, have had a profound effect on our lives is simply wrong. Just imagine suggesting that *Picture Post* or *Time* or LIFE had as much impact on our lives as *Das Kapital, Mein Kampf* or the Bible... Photographs can be very beautiful, informative, ugly or anything else the photographer chooses to show. Photographs can definitely inspire us, but the written word has the ability to spark the imagination to greater depths than any photograph, whose content is limited to what exists in the frame." Mr. Haruni is, by the way, a documentary photographer.

His argument forced us to once again confront our premise. We compared Mr. Haruni's thoughts and those of other respondents and finally determined: A collection of pictures that "changed the world" is a thing worth contemplating, if only to arrive at some resolution about the influential nature of photography and whether it is limited, vast or in between. We do not claim that LIFE's 100 are *the* 100 or the *top* 100, but that they, and the other related landmark images presented here, argue on behalf of the power of pictures.

Not every iconic image will be found here. Many nominated the 1937 crash of the *Hindenburg.* We looked hard at the picture, the event and the aftermath, and decided against. We may be remiss about the *Hindenburg,* and we may be wrong about excluding our friend Alfred Eisenstaedt's picture of the sailor kissing the nurse in Times Square. Some of you will, no doubt, be disappointed by some choices and omissions. But many who answered our query will be pleased to see their passions shared. "The lone Chinese demonstrator as he stops a column of advancing tanks in Beijing was a person of steel," wrote Maek Lester S. Cayabyab, a journalism student in Manila. Jacob Meade, a "photo fan" from Amherst, N.H., won't find his *Hindenburg,* but he offered a compelling argument for "the portrait of Anne Frank: The poignancy of her gaze haunts the world to this day, pointing up the horror of Hitler's genocide and making us wonder how many brilliant young women such as herself were lost."

We took all nominations seriously, added our own, and then solicited the advice of some old LIFE hands. Renowned photographers such as John Loengard and Gordon Parks (who passed away in 2006 but who, three years earlier, not only offered his opinions but wrote for us the evocative introduction immediately following) contributed their expertise. And then we made our final choices, and wrote our rationales in the captions.

This book gained instant success back in 2003. It was lauded as a considered and provocative look at the history of photography, and seen as a passionate defense for the art form's vitality in the modern age. In the years immediately following its publication, we at LIFE saw this vitality being confirmed over and over: as a basis of evidence in the Middle East turmoil and from the mountains of Mars, as a new way to communicate via the sending of a trillion cell phone images. It became clear to us that it was time to revisit *100 Photographs That Changed the World.* We decided that our original argument—which is to say, our original book—remained durable, but some freshening would make it even better.

So that, dear reader, is the premise behind these pictures, then and now. We hope you enjoy this look back—and forward.

This **Rare** Collection

An essay, poetry and pictures
by Gordon Parks

In 2003, LIFE *asked one of our longtime friends and associates, the storied photographer, filmmaker, painter, writer and poet Gordon Parks, to provide the introduction to this special volume. Happily, Mr. Parks consented, and crafted an essay both moving and characteristically selfless. Then we went back to Mr. Parks and asked him to meditate just a bit further on any of his own images that might have effected change. He chose two. When Mr. Parks's portrait of Ella Watson, a government cleaning woman in Washington, D.C., was published in 1942, it focused attention on continuing inequities in the land of the free. And when he produced a story in 1961 on Flavio da Silva, an impoverished 12-year-old dying in a favela in Rio, a flood of contributions washed over Flavio and his family. The boy lived. Gordon himself, an American treasure and a LIFE legend, died in 2006 at age 93.*

Change has spread itself graciously over the centuries. Mankind, living in the middle of this vast uncertain space, has always been around to record the light, or darkness, hovering over it—but even during the very darkest of times, change somehow manages to arrive, leaving us in awe. Bewildering, at times enlightening, change moves in to alter the course of our lives.

Without doubt, words have helped influence universal thought and action. As was cited in the précis on the opposite page, a glance back to the words in the Bible, the Koran, the Magna Carta or the Declaration of Independence instantly proves the point. Sculptors and painters, with their particular poetry, have also established new attitudes down through the years.

But I have come to believe that no art form transforms human apathy quicker than that of photography. Having absorbed the message of a memorable photograph, the viewer's sense of compassion and newfound wisdom come together like two lips touching. And it is an extraordinary thing when an unforgettable photograph propels you from an evil interlude to the conviction that there must come a better day.

Let us give thought to those who distinguish themselves with cameras. They are no ordinary lot. In publications, they don't show up as the heroes, but they are the ones who put themselves in the position to find the memorable images of the maimed or dead, and thus try to help pull together a broken world. Hoping to make that world weary of disasters, certain photographers attack scenes of overwhelming emotion. They allow their cameras to become swords in their hands. When scanning the pages ahead, one should not grow tired of witnessing these things—corpses stacked, awaiting the fire of a Holocaust oven; two young black lynch victims, dead before a cheerful white mob; a Viet Cong guerrilla, his eyes tightly shut, grimacing as a policeman fires a bullet into his head—for that is the photographer's charge to us, that we never forget. Recalling such shocking tragedies makes our thoughts burn as if doused with oil, and we no longer walk around forgetful. We remember the black hours with fury and shame, and we are changed. The cameras keep watch as mankind goes on filling the universe with its behavior, and they change us.

The photographs that take their rightful place in this rare collection come wrapped in a kind of mystery. Perhaps providence intended these things to be photographed, at just that instant. Or maybe the camera lenses that captured these instances on these particular days did so purely by chance. This mystery applies equally to a photograph recording the moment the Beatles arrive in New York City as it does to that when pro-

American Gothic

I'm tired of everything.
I'm tired of waking up
and remembering things
I know I oughta forget,
and of smellin' food
too rich for my cupboard
or those plates on my table.
I ain't crying about nothin'.
That's just how things are.
I'm alive and movin' around
and my toe nails keep growin'.
So weepin's a waste of time.
I just hope time ain't growin' tired
of hanging around here with me.

testers were slammed against brick walls by the water from high-pressure hoses.

As to the cruel imagery, that which was born in darkness, I have a curious question: What sorts of feelings grasped the photographers' hearts as they recorded the horrible scenes? The options, ranging from pangs of sorrow to shocking numbness to awe to despair to anger, are plentiful. Perhaps their reactions depended upon where their own lives had been or where their lives were going. How did they do it? For the execution of any of these photographs, a finger and an instinct joined forces for a split second. The combat photographer's life, clothed in danger and uncertainty, might vanish in any moment. How did they do it? Larry Burrows, Robert Capa and all the many others who have perished in war zones could speak with authority on this question, but they chose instead to speak to us with their cameras, telling us how certain men have murdered

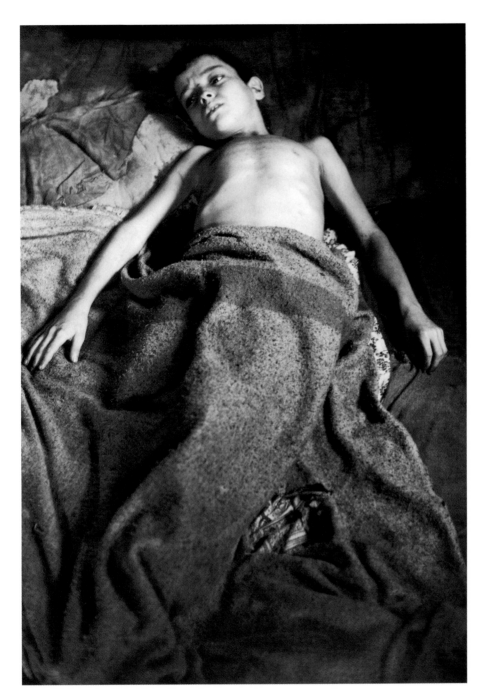

Flavio

From stony heights I first saw him
climbing beneath cloudless clouds
floating the mountain's hot air.
His face, shrunken by furious hunger,
was colored with amber and honey.
His neck, akin to a leaning tower,
was drowning in rivers of sweat.
Time had screwed his broom-stick legs
into his bony disgruntled feet.
There, with death hiding inside him
at the mid-point of blistering day,
he smiled a smile I'll never forget.
Then, on a mountainside of silence,
Flavio da Silva became my friend.

other men over a bucket of dirty drinking water.

If you were to ask me to explain my own absence from some of these places, I would say, "Maybe I should have been there, but I'm glad I was not there. I loathe photographing death." But we are fortunate that others were there for the terrible moments as well as the good, because as we look at their pictures an indisputably important fact emerges: These images helped push us toward a change.

You might say the world still suffers gunfire and terrorist bloodletting, that there is still smoke everywhere. But take another glance at these photographs. The cameras have observed our lives in order to get us to tomorrow. The cameras have observed our lives in search of hope. Photography, as it appears in this memorable collection, nourishes hope. Without hope, contentment is impossible in our world.

The Arts

Pigeon House and Barn 1827

As early as 1793, Frenchman Nicéphore Niépce and his brother Claude imagined a photographic process, and over the next several years, Nicéphore experimented with various light-sensitive substances and cameras. In 1824 he produced a view from his window on a metal plate covered with asphalt. That and most other pictures fashioned by Niépce in the 1820s no longer exist, but the fuzzy image of a pigeon house and a barn roof taken in the summer of 1827 is a good representation of Niépce's art. To make what he called a "heliograph," or sun drawing, Niépce employed an exposure time of more than eight hours. Photography, if not yet practical, had been invented.

Photograph by **Nicéphore Niépce**

Another Landmark Image

British philosopher and scientist William Henry Fox Talbot was a dabbler of renown. In 1833, while on holiday in Italy, he wondered if images his camera threw against paper could be made to imprint themselves. Talbot's experiments led to the first paper negatives and greatly reduced the exposure time required to make a picture.

Lacock Abbey, 1835
Photograph by **William Henry Fox Talbot**
National Museum of Photography, Film & Television

A Still Life 1837

In 1826, Parisian stage designer Louis Daguerre learned of Nicéphore Niépce's heliography and promptly importuned Niépce to share his ideas. The men partnered in 1829, but Niépce died in '33. By 1837, Daguerre had developed a process by which an image could be frozen with exposures of minutes rather than hours. The daguerreotype led to a boom in photography; in an 1840 magazine account, Edgar Allan Poe said it "must undoubtedly be regarded as the most important, and perhaps the most extraordinary triumph of modern science."

Photograph by **Louis Daguerre**

An Autochrome 1909

Early efforts to render photographs in color, at first using plates coated with silver chloride, date to 1848; they were generally unsuccessful. Two decades later, drawing from ideas about color decomposition forwarded by Scottish scientist James Clerk Maxwell, Louis Ducos du Hauron made a color picture by superimposing three photos of one subject, shot through different filters. It was left to the Lumière brothers, famous as pioneering filmmakers, to develop a single-plate color process, which they did in 1904. Below: a Paris aircraft exhibit shot in Autochrome, the Lumière method.

Photograph by **Léon Gimple** Société Française de Photographie, Paris

Uncut Sheet of Cartes de Visite c. 1860

In the 1850s, the calling card changed when *cartes de visite*—2 ¹/₂" by 4" albumen prints mounted on cards—became de rigueur in French society, then in the U.S. "Card portraits, as everybody knows, have become the social currency, the 'green-backs' of civilization," wrote Oliver Wendell Holmes in 1863. The photo ID is a must-have for coming and going in today's world.

Photograph by **André Adolphe Disdéri** Gernsheim Collection, The University of Texas at Austin

Sarah Bernhardt 1864

The Divine Sarah was but 20, and just on her way to becoming one of the theater's immortals, when she persuaded the French photographer Nadar to preserve her delicate beauty on film. Nadar's Parisian studio was a magnet for such luminaries as Baudelaire and Delacroix, who wanted to pose in the informal Nadar manner. Of course, those seeking fame would ever more find the camera irresistible, except, perhaps, when paparazzi became so intrusive as to menace. The need to be photographed and the apparent human need to see these photos has led to the present, disturbing cult of celebrity.

Photograph by **Nadar**

STEINWAY HALL. [FROM A PHOTOGRAPH BY PACH.]

First Printed Photograph

1873

The halftone process to print photos was used for the first time in America in New York's *Daily Graphic:* The subject was Manhattan's Steinway Hall. Newspaper photography, static at the outset, grew to become the liveliest part of many journals, and in 1942 its importance was officially recognized in the U.S. when the Pulitzer Prize board began citing photos as well as reportage in its journalism-awards program. That year, a photograph of a fight on the picket line during a 1941 United Auto Workers' strike at a Ford plant in Detroit won the prize, and since then, Pulitzers have gone to pictures depicting racism, crime, poverty, heroism, terrorism and war, among other things.

Photograph from The New York Daily Graphic

Other Landmark Images

How photographs might be conveyed—and how quickly—became a question almost as soon as they were reproduced. In 1935 this photograph of a plane crash in the Adirondacks was sent from New York to 25 other cities, and Associated Press Wirephoto was born. The '30s saw a boom in mass media photography, as transmitted images let people see within hours what they previously only imagined from newspaper or radio accounts, and new magazines like LIFE and *Look* showed Americans scenes from faraway lands within a week. That was one revolution, and then another was cell phone and digital photography.
On this page we see what is credited as the first-ever picture taken and transmitted from a phone, made by technology entrepreneur Philippe Kahn of his newborn baby daughter Sophie on June 11, 1997, in Santa Cruz, California, and sent instantly to 2,000 relations, friends and associates around the globe. Kahn was a proud papa in more ways than he realized: Not only did the camera phone (and otherwise transmitted digital photography) become an underpinning of the modern phenomenon known as social networking, it became a crucial communication and political tool. Pictures sent from inside rallies and riots in totalitarian regimes spoke truth to power in a nanosecond. There were no more secrets.

First Wirephoto, 1935
Photograph from AP

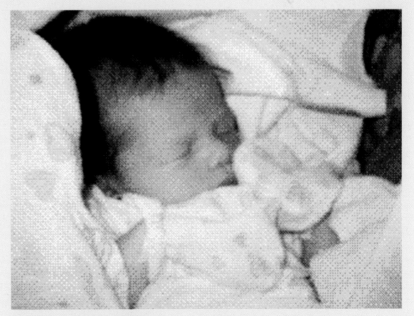

First Camera Phone Photo
Photograph by **Philippe Kahn**, Courtesy of memo.com

An Oasis in the Badlands
1905

When this picture was taken, the vast majority of easterners in the United States were of European heritage. Their view of Indians in the American West was, by and large, contemptuous, considering them little more than inferior obstacles. When the photographs of Edward Curtis appeared, most people were entirely unprepared for the obvious dignity and humanity of these native Americans. Here, Red Hawk, an Oglala Sioux, is clad in tribal garb as his horse drinks on the plains of South Dakota.

Photograph by
Edward S. Curtis
N.Y. Public Library

Gertrude Vanderbilt Whitney 1913

The earliest fashion photography consisted mostly of portraits of stylish aristocrats, and the first fashion photographer of note was Baron Adolphe de Meyer, who was hired to shoot for *Vogue* in 1913, the year he took this picture. In the '20s, the tradition of the artistically adventurous, stylized fashion photograph began in earnest when such as Edward Steichen and the art deco–influenced George Hoyningen-Huene entered the game. That tradition remained strong from Man Ray and Horst P. Horst through to the Avedons of today.

Photograph by **Baron Adolphe de Meyer** Vogue, Conde Nast/Corbis

Another Landmark Image

France and England quarreled about many things through the centuries, but in certain areas they were not competitive, nor would they ever be. Immutable truth held that the English would always make a better ale, the French a better wine. London could do a splendid tea but could mount no challenge to Paree when it came to fine cuisine or haute couture. Then, in the mid-1960s, Mary Quant introduced the miniskirt at her Carnaby Street boutique, and soon the mods of London, personified by a skinny teenage model called Twiggy, were setting the standards in style.

Twiggy, 1967 Photograph from Dalmas/Sipa

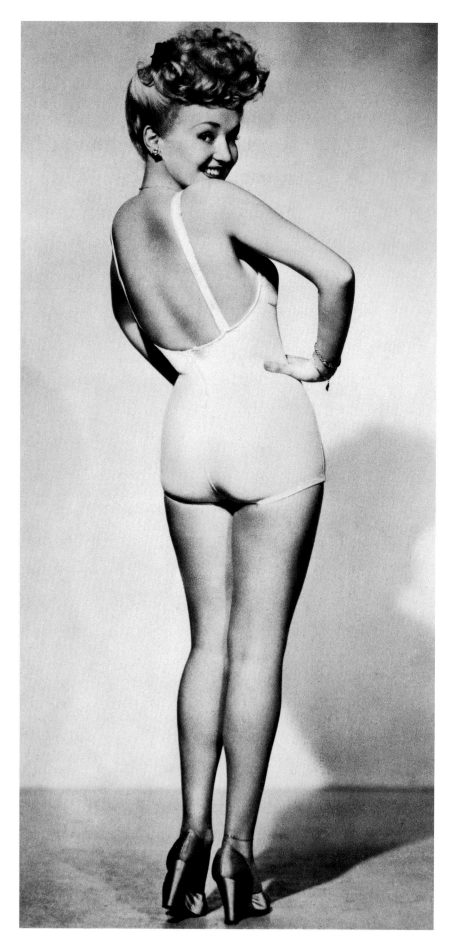

Betty Grable
1942

World War II took American boys to far-flung places and some rough duty. For many, mail came infrequently at best, and at times it held only a Dear John letter. The troops were desperate for some link to home, some reminder of what they were fighting for. Betty Grable and her million-dollar legs were the perfect balm for what ailed 'em, and this 1942 pinup of the easygoing girl with oodles of back-home charm, and other assets, made the war seem a little more bearable. Sexy pinups later grew to poster size, perhaps most memorably in the endlessly reproduced portrait of Farrah Fawcett.

Photograph distributed by 20th Century Fox

Che Guevara 1960

Cuban revolutionary Ernesto "Che" Guevara had just been killed in Bolivia in 1967 when, as if on cue, this epitomic portrait of a left-wing firebrand was released to the world in many forms, especially posters. Its romantic bravado captured the hearts and minds of young people everywhere. Korda's photo *Guerrillero Heroico* had been taken in 1960 at a service for slain Cuban revolutionaries, and Korda later gave the picture to an Italian publisher who, after Guevara's death, made it into a poster. If Grable's is the archetypal pinup, then Guevara's, which sold millions, is the quintessential poster. Korda never got a penny.

Photograph by **Alberto Korda** Courtesy Couturier Gallery, Los Angeles

Dead Sea Scrolls 1947

This picture stands for a library's worth of images that illustrate photography's power and reach today. In 1947 the first of the Dead Sea Scrolls, written between 200 B.C. and 68 A.D., were found near Jerusalem. By 1956, pieces of 870 scrolls had been discovered in 11 caves. It was clear that the scrolls, which contained much from the Hebrew Bible but also new prophecies and psalms, could illuminate Old Testament scholarship and perhaps early Christianity. But for decades, the scrolls were withheld from the public and even most scholars. Then, in 1991, the Huntington Library in California said that it would allow access to its microfilm files of all scroll photographs.

Photograph by **Larry Burrows**

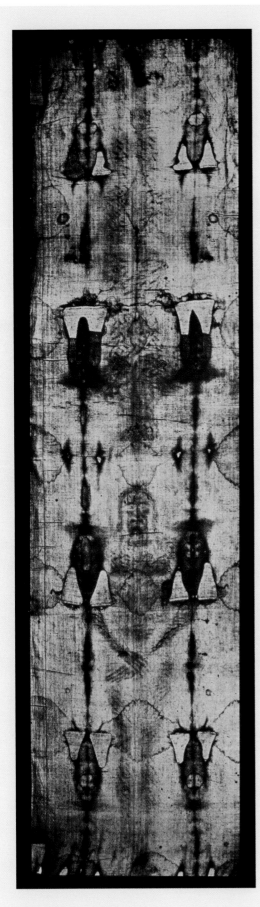

Other Landmark Images

Without entering into the debate as to whether the Shroud of Turin is the authentic burial cloth of Jesus Christ or a fake manufactured centuries later, it is true that the Shroud has moved many—and has reached and impressed millions throughout the world—because of the science of photography. The shadowy image on the Shroud is difficult to discern as human; in fact, the closer you get to the Shroud, the harder the task becomes. But when seen in a photographic negative, the face, hands, beard and other details of a man are immediately, stunningly distinct.

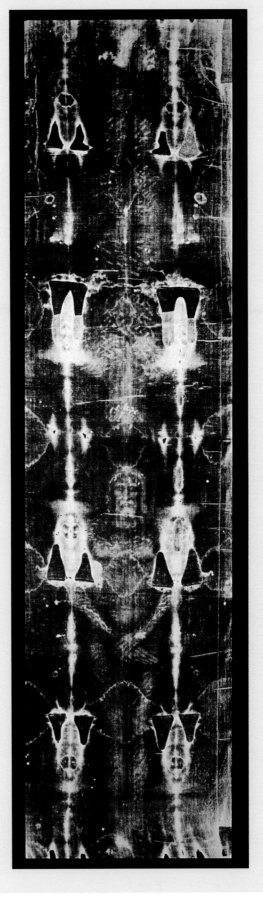

Positive and Negative Photographs of the Shroud of Turin, 1982
Photograph by
Vernon Miller

Photographic Art

Ever since Daguerre first composed a still life, photography has had the dual purpose of not only recording a scene but also of rendering it. As with painters, there have been, down through the decades, masters of the photographic medium, stylists whose work thrills and inspires us. The Roman poet Horace said, "A picture is a poem without words," and the aesthetes of the camera are stellar exemplars of this sentiment.

Julia Margaret Cameron
Call, I Follow, I Follow,
Let Me Die! **c. 1867**

The Victorian-era portraitist considered herself, rather than a photographer, an artist who made pictures. Influenced by pre-Raphaelite painters, she produced soft-focus images that are beautiful and beguiling.

Eugène Atget
Organ Player
and Singing Girl
1898

A frustrated actor,
Atget considered
turning to
painting. But he
took up the
camera instead
and quickly
showed himself
to be a genius of
composition. For
30 years, Atget's
grail was to
capture all that
was picturesque
in the city he
loved, Paris.

Edward Steichen
The Flatiron,
Evening **1905**

He did portraits,
landscapes, fashion
photography, even
advertising work,
all of it marked by
by a strong sense
of design.

**Jacques-Henri
Lartigue**
Bichonnade in
Flight **1905**

Given a camera at
eight, the French
boy wasn't yet a
teen when he took
this typically gay,
bright, airy picture.

Man Ray

Black and White, Paris 1926

An early devotee of Dada and Surrealism, he took up photography to pay for his painting. Experimenting tirelessly, he used the camera in wildly exciting ways, and was a master of fashion and portrait photography.

Henri Cartier-Bresson
The Decisive Moment **1952**

A sharpshooter with a 35mm, he "prowled the streets . . . determined to trap life, to preserve life in the act of living." One of the foremost photojournalists, his pictures were crisp, essential, insightful, artful.

Magnum

Society

Glasgow 1868

When Glasgow's City Improvement Trust wanted a photographer to document condemned slums, they picked Thomas Annan, a portrait artist who rejected the typical props of the day. (He even converted a hansom cab into a darkroom.) Annan was among the very first to chronicle the life of the urban poor in photos such as the one below. Critics say he concentrated more on buildings than on the souls within, but his images tell a clear, sad tale.

Photograph by **Thomas Annan**
International Museum of Photography, George Eastman House

New York City c. 1880

Muckrakers were busy on both sides of the Atlantic in the late 1800s. While Annan was chronicling Glasgow and John Thomson was exposing the down-and-out in his *Street Life in London,* Jacob Riis was cataloguing the lives of "street arabs," nomadic children in New York City who had been abandoned or neglected in ways people are ashamed to treat dogs today. Riis's *How the Other Half Lives,* a sensation in 1890, remains a classic.

Photograph by **Jacob Riis**
The Jacob A. Riis Collection, Museum of the City of New York

Abraham Lincoln 1860

Mathew Brady took this picture on February 27, 1860, the day Abraham Lincoln gave a rousing antislavery speech at a New York City institute known as Cooper Union. The photo and the speech were then widely circulated during Honest Abe's presidential campaign. Brady, who claimed his portrait won Lincoln the election, said he made the tall man look less gangly through the sophistry of pulling Lincoln's collar high to make his neck look shorter. Brady went further, by removing some of the great man's deep facial furrows and doctoring his drifting left eye. The President himself recognized the importance of the photo: "Brady and the Cooper Institute made me President." This print was the humble progenitor of today's image-based political campaigns.

Photograph by
Mathew Brady

Other Landmark Images

Brady's wizardry may have saved the day for Lincoln, but for two pols in the 1988 election, pictures proved their undoing. Gary Hart, a Colorado Democrat, was a front-runner for his party's nomination when *The Miami Herald* ran this photo of the married man and model Donna Rice, taken during a cruise on the *Monkey Business*. A week later, Hart dropped out of the race. The field open, Michael Dukakis, governor of Massachusetts, became the Democratic choice against George Bush. At a General Dynamics plant in Michigan, the Duke wanted to show he wasn't soft on defense, so he took a spin in a tank. Compared with WWII pilot Bush, the little Dukakis came off a clown. To firmly seal the deal, Bush supporters ran ads featuring the visage of Willie Horton, a hardened con who, while at liberty under the Massachusetts "weekend pass" program, had committed rape.

Michael Dukakis, 1988
Photograph from AP

Gary Hart and Donna Rice, Bimini, 1987
Photograph by **The National Enquirer** Getty

Willie Horton, 1987
Photograph from AP/Lawrence Eagle Tribune

SURRAT.   BOOTH.   HAROLD.

War Department, Washington, April 20, 1865,

 # $100,000 REWARD!

THE MURDERER

Of our late beloved President, Abraham Lincoln,

IS STILL AT LARGE.

$50,000 REWARD

Will be paid by this Department for his apprehension, in addition to any reward offered by Municipal Authorities or State Executives.

$25,000 REWARD

Will be paid for the apprehension of JOHN H. SURRATT, one of Booth's Accomplices.

$25,000 REWARD

Will be paid for the apprehension of David C. Harold, another of Booth's accomplices.

LIBERAL REWARDS will be paid for any information that shall conduce to the arrest of either of the above-named criminals, or their accomplices.

All persons harboring or secreting the said persons, or either of them, or aiding or assisting their concealment or escape, will be treated as accomplices in the murder of the President and the attempted assassination of the Secretary of State, and shall be subject to trial before a Military Commission and the punishment of DEATH.

Let the stain of innocent blood be removed from the land by the arrest and punishment of the murderers.

All good citizens are exhorted to aid public justice on this occasion. Every man should consider his own conscience charged with this solemn duty, and rest neither night nor day until it be accomplished.

EDWIN M. STANTON, Secretary of War.

DESCRIPTIONS.—BOOTH is Five Feet 7 or 8 inches high, slender build, high forehead, black hair, black eyes, and wears a heavy black moustache.

JOHN H. SURRAT is about 5 feet, 9 inches. Hair rather thin and dark; eyes rather light; no beard. Would weigh 145 or 150 pounds. Complexion rather pale and clear, with color in his cheeks. Wore light clothes of fine quality. Shoulders square; cheek bones rather prominent; chin narrow; ears projecting at the top; forehead rather low and square, but broad. Parts his hair on the right side; neck rather long. His lips are firmly set. A slim man.

DAVID C. HAROLD is five feet six inches high, hair dark, eyes dark, eyebrows rather heavy, full face, nose short, hand short and fleshy, feet small, instep high, round bodied, naturally quick and active, slightly closes his eyes when looking at a person.

NOTICE.—In addition to the above, State and other authorities have offered rewards amounting to almost one hundred thousand dollars, making an aggregate of about TWO HUNDRED THOUSAND DOLLARS.

Six days after the assassination of Abraham Lincoln, in the midst of a frantic two-week search, the War Department hung Wanted posters with an innovation: Pasted on were photographs of John Wilkes Booth and two of his suspected conspirators. After seeing Booth's picture, fishermen pointed soldiers in the right direction, and they located the assassin in a Virginia tobacco barn; they burned the barn and found the suspect had been shot through the neck. This Wanted poster proved so effective that using a photograph became a fixture of law enforcement.

Photographer Unknown

Passport
1914

Passports date to 450 B.C., but France's King Louis XIV popularized them when he personally signed requests that his subjects be given safe passage through ports, or *passe port*. By the mid-1800s, growing masses of travelers were overwhelming authorities, and countries stopped issuing the documents. With the advent of World War I, nations started demanding them again. In 1914 the United States began requiring a passport photo, turning the once whimsical ID portrait—the charming *carte de visite*—into a grim instrument of official identification. Who could have guessed in 1916 that a certificate for transit such as this one, which belonged to the famous, globe-trotting dancer Isadora Duncan, would one day be a staple of American—indeed, global—life?

Copied by Brad Trent

Promontory Point 1869

The ceremony begins on May 10, 1869, as an eastbound Central Pacific locomotive and a westbound Union Pacific locomotive meet in Promontory Point, Utah, marking the completion of the first transcontinental railroad. The men on the cowcatchers are ready to toast the driving of the golden spike. The work had been brutal. At one stage, efforts to tunnel through the marble spine of a Sierra Nevada mountain consumed an entire year, as only eight inches a day of progress was possible. So: a fabulous accomplishment. But this is also an early example of a photo op—the use of a picture as a means to an end. Folks back East could see, plain as day, that a train could take them all the way to California, where businessmen anxiously awaited their commerce.

Photograph by
Charles Phelps Cushing

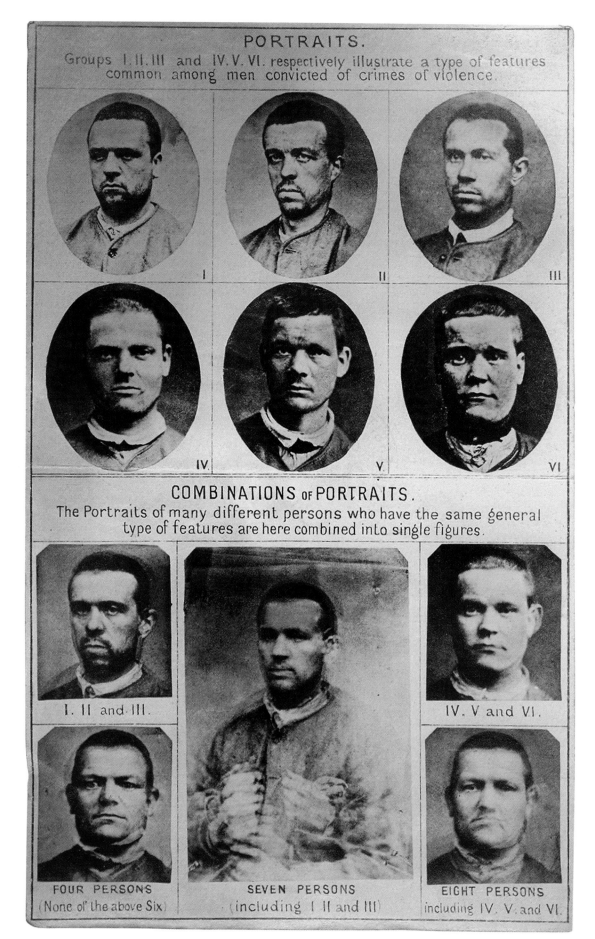

PORTRAITS.

Groups I. II. III and IV. V. VI. respectively illustrate a type of features common among men convicted of crimes of violence.

I

II

III

IV

V

VI

COMBINATIONS OF PORTRAITS.

The Portraits of many different persons who have the same general type of features are here combined into single figures.

I. II and III.

IV. V and VI.

FOUR PERSONS
(None of the above Six)

SEVEN PERSONS
(including I. II and III)

EIGHT PERSONS
including IV. V. and VI.

Eugenics
c. 1890

The highborn Englishman Francis Galton, a cousin of Charles Darwin, was the father of eugenics, an unsavory and ultimately fatal misunderstanding of hereditary traits that had a strong vogue in the Victorian era before the term "genetics" was coined. Derived from the Greek word meaning "wellborn," eugenics maintained that genius, strength and other physical characteristics, as well as various weaknesses and a propensity for crime, were not only inherited but discernible. Galton, who was knighted in 1909, said that "a highly gifted race of men" could be produced through selective breeding, and that those unfit for procreation should refrain or be regarded as "enemies to the State, and to have forfeited all claims to kindness." Galton also believed in photography's ability to tell absolute truth. Many found his composite images of criminal types persuasive.

Photograph by
Francis Galton
Courtesy Special Collections, University College, London

Another Landmark Image

Eugenics traveled well, gathering adherents from India and Japan to the U.S., Canada and, especially, Germany. American eugenicists had by the late 1920s successfully lobbied for laws mandating sterilization of the "unfit" in 24 states. In Germany, Dr. Alfred Ploetz's Society for Racial Hygiene, founded in 1905, opposed charitable programs to protect the ill, and approved of infanticide of the weak. In 1910, Sir Francis Galton graciously received Ploetz in London. Later, Ploetz ardently backed Hitler. It took something as dire as the Holocaust to destroy the credibility of eugenics.

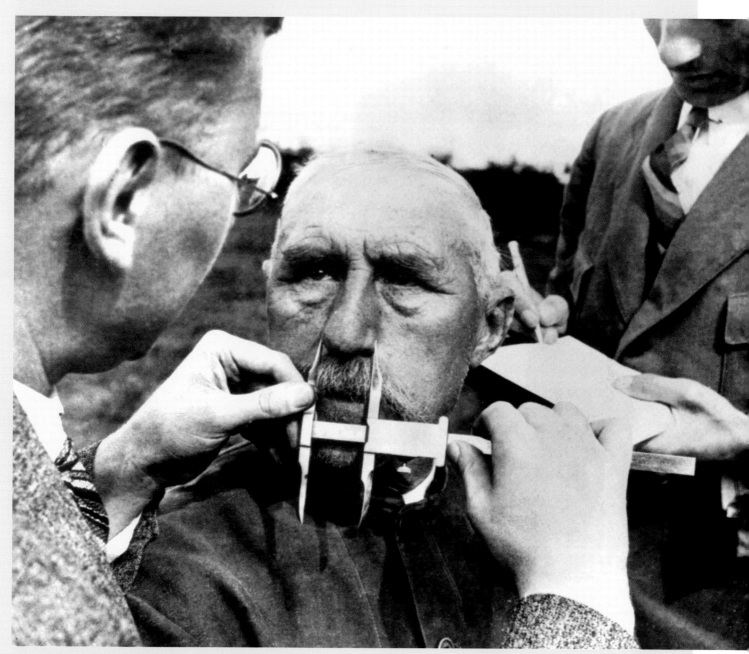

Aryan Race Determination Tests, Germany, c. 1940
Photograph by **Henry Guttmann** Hulton Archive/Getty

Flight 1903

On December 17, 1903, two bicycle mechanics from Ohio realized one of humanity's wildest dreams: For 12 seconds they were possessed of true flight. Before the day ended, Orville and Wilbur Wright would keep their wood-wire-and-cloth *Flyer* aloft for 59 seconds. Sober citizens knew that only birds used wings to take to the air, so without being at the site, near Kitty Hawk, N.C., or seeing this photo, few would have believed the Wrights' story. Although it had taken ages for humans to fly, once the brothers made their breakthrough, the learning curve reached the heavens. Within 15 years of this critical moment, nearly all the elements of the modern airplane had been imagined, if not yet developed.

Photograph from Library of Congress

Another Landmark Image

The world became a much smaller place on May 21, 1927, when Charles Lindbergh, a.k.a. the Flying Fool, touched down in France after crossing the Atlantic alone and nonstop. To spur himself, the modest midwesterner chanted en route, "There's no alternative but death and failure." A victory tour took Lucky Lindy to London, where he and the *Spirit of St. Louis* were greeted by 150,000 admirers at Croydon Aerodrome (below). Long-distance commercial aviation would soon alter human movement.

Charles Lindbergh, Croydon Aerodrome, England, 1927
Photograph from Brown Brothers

Breaker Boys
1910

What Charles Dickens did with words for the underage toilers of London, Lewis Hine did with photographs for the youthful laborers in the United States. In 1908 the National Child Labor Committee was already campaigning to put the nation's two million young workers back in school when the group hired Hine. The Wisconsin native traveled to half the states, capturing images of children working in mines, mills and on the streets. Here he has photographed "breaker boys," whose job was to separate coal from slate, in South Pittston, Pa. Once again, pictures swayed the public in a way cold statistics had not, and the country enacted laws banning child labor.

Photograph by **Lewis W. Hine**
National Archives

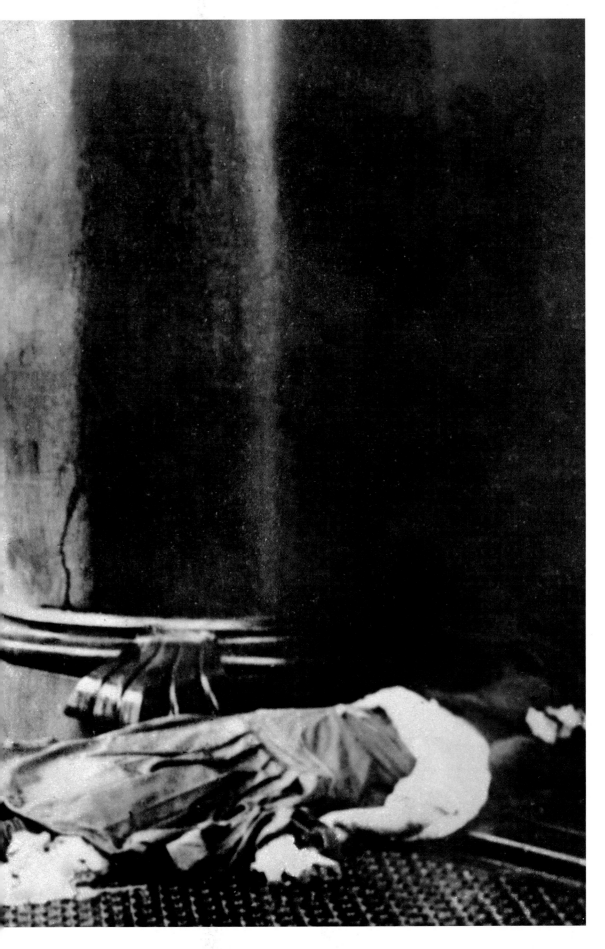

Triangle Shirtwaist Company Fire
1911

The Triangle Shirtwaist Company always kept its doors locked to ensure that the young immigrant women stayed stooped over their machines and didn't steal anything. When a fire broke out on Saturday, March 25, 1911, on the eighth floor of the New York City factory, the locks sealed the workers' fate. In just 30 minutes, 146 were killed. Witnesses thought the owners were tossing their best fabric out the windows to save it, then realized workers were jumping, sometimes after sharing a kiss (the scene can be viewed now as an eerie precursor to the World Trade Center events of September, 11, 2001, only a mile and a half south). The Triangle disaster spurred a national crusade for workplace safety.

Photograph by
Brown Brothers

Trampled by the King's Horse 1913

By the 19th century, it finally became a public issue that females were not allowed to participate in national elections. The struggle for woman suffrage took many forms but often played out as an exercise in civil disobedience, in the U.K. and U.S. especially. Emily Davison was born in England in 1872 and graduated from London University. By 1909 she was immersed in women's rights to the extent that she was repeatedly imprisoned, then released after hunger strikes. In 1913, before half a million people, she threw herself at Anmer, the king's horse that was running in the Epsom Derby, in a final, fatal act of protest. Many thought her insane. Others considered her a martyr.

Photograph from Hulton Archive/Getty

Another Landmark Image

The Title IX legislation of 1972, which banned sexual discrimination in education programs receiving federal funds, led to a boom in schoolgirl sports. When a U.S. team of women raised on Title IX won the 1999 soccer World Cup final, still more girls were inspired to lace up their sneakers. Brandi Chastain said that she ripped off her shirt in celebration because guys had been doing it for years.

Brandi Chastain, 1999
Photograph by **Robert Beck** Sports Illustrated

Lynching 1930

A mob of 10,000 whites took sledgehammers to the county jailhouse doors to get at these two young blacks accused of raping a white girl; the girl's uncle saved the life of a third by proclaiming the man's innocence. Although this was Marion, Ind., most of the nearly 5,000 lynchings documented between Reconstruction and the late 1960s were perpetrated in the South. (Hangings, beatings and mutilations were called the sentence of "Judge Lynch.") Some lynching photos were made into postcards designed to boost white supremacy, but the tortured bodies and grotesquely happy crowds ended up revolting as many as they scared. Today the images remind us that we have not come as far from barbarity as we'd like to think.

Photograph by **Lawrence Beitler** Bettmann/Corbis

Another Landmark Image

Blacks had been taking it on the chin in America for a long time. But that didn't stop most all of America, black and white, from cheering when Joe Louis knocked out Max Schmeling at Yankee Stadium in 1938. The German, Hitler's favorite, had beaten Louis two years earlier, but this time the Brown Bomber took revenge 2:04 into the fight. The hypocrisy of a nation honoring a black man for beating an Aryan, yet persecuting his brethren, was lost on too many.

Louis Knocks Out Schmeling, 1938
Photograph from AP

Bonnie and Clyde 1933

The Depression was in full swing in the early '30s, and its Grim Reaper's scythe cut a terrible swathe through Middle America. Farmers lost their fields, and families their homes; the banks would wait only so long before foreclosing. It was a perfect incubator for crime, and if the likes of John Dillinger and Pretty Boy Floyd stole from the banks, and maybe some mortgage papers got destroyed along the way, well, that didn't bother folks much. Many of the antiheroes assumed a Robin Hood persona, and their styles were widely imitated. Here, America's favorite crime couple, Bonnie Parker and Clyde Barrow, strike a pose.

Photograph from the Granger Collection

Migrant Mother 1936

This California farmworker, age 32, had just sold her tent and the tires off her car to buy food for her seven kids. The family was living on scavenged vegetables and wild birds. Working for the federal government, Dorothea Lange took pictures like this one to document how the Depression colluded with the Dust Bowl to ravage lives. Along with the writing of her economist husband, Paul Taylor, Lange's work helped convince the public and the government of the need to help field hands. Lange later said that this woman, whose name she did not ask, "seemed to know that my pictures might help her, and so she helped me."

Photograph by
Dorothea Lange
Library of Congress

Roger Bannister
1954

There are certain givens for people, certain things we know we just can't do. In 1954, it was gospel to one and all that a human being simply could not cover a one-mile distance in less than four minutes. It was impossible. To John Landy, who had run 4:02 a few times, it was "like a wall." The one nonbeliever was a British medical student who took up track while studying at Oxford and developed scientific training regimes to try to achieve the unachievable. On May 6, Roger Bannister ran the mile in 3:59.4. His historic portrait made front pages around the globe, and his feat redefined what was possible. Two months later, in a changed world, Landy, too, broke the unbreakable four-minute mile.

Photograph from AP

Other Landmark Images

Twenty-year-old Kathy Switzer crashes the men-only 1967 Boston Marathon, and race official Jock Semple tries to run her off the course—then promptly gets bounced for his trouble by Switzer's boyfriend, Tom Miller. The photos ran worldwide, along with the news that Switzer finished the 26.2-mile race. Women kept the heat on in Boston, and five years later they were allowed to compete. In 1984 the women's Olympic marathon debuted in Los Angeles.

The Boston Marathon, 1967
Photographs from AP

Jackie Robinson 1955

Everything he did in his Brooklyn Dodgers uniform was electrifying, designed to keep the opposition off-balance, ill at ease, on the defensive. It was a mirror image to everything society was laying on him, every pitch, every game, every morning, every night, every day of his life. The first black major leaguer had to turn the other cheek, and it made him tired but tougher; it made him a bigger man, but to a lot of whites and to every black he was already bigger than life, this person who tore himself apart that others might someday find completeness. Here, in the third game of the 1955 World Series, Jackie Robinson terrorizes the Yankees en route to a world championship.

Photograph by **Ralph Morse**

Another Landmark Image

Sports can transcend the arena. Jesse Owens embarrassed Hitler in 1936. In a 1956 Olympic water polo match held only a month after the U.S.S.R. sent 200,000 troops to quash a Hungarian revolt, Hungary beat the Soviet Union every which way; the violent game was halted with Hungary ahead 4–0. And at the 1980 Winter Games, a bunch of scrappy college kids and recent grads from across America pulled together to defeat the mighty Soviet machine 4–3 in a thrilling ice hockey game. There was more than just the usual cold war tension in the air: In late 1979 the U.S.S.R. had invaded Afghanistan, and U.S. President Jimmy Carter was already talking about a boycott of the upcoming Moscow Olympics. Carter made good on his threat in the summer of 1980, and the Soviets returned the favor by forgoing the 1984 Games in Los Angeles.

U.S.A. vs. U.S.S.R., 1980
Photograph by
Heinz Kluetmeier
Sports Illustrated

Massacre at Sharpeville 1960

To control the passage of blacks through white areas, South African law required them to carry a passbook at all times. On March 21, some 20,000 gathered in the township of Sharpeville to protest the rule. Police opened fire, killing 69 and injuring some 180, most of them shot in the back as they tried to flee. Said Police Commander D.H. Pienaar, "If they do these things, they must learn their lessons the hard way." This image of random carnage forced other nations to heed the vile injustices there.

Photograph from Hulton Archive/Getty

Another Landmark Image

The world recoiled in 1976 upon seeing this photo of 13-year-old Hector Peterson, slain by South African police during protests in Soweto.

Hector Peterson, Soweto, 1976
Photograph from AP

Johnson Is Sworn In 1963

Lyndon Baines Johnson takes the presidential oath of office on November 22 as *Air Force One* carries his wife, Lady Bird, Jacqueline Kennedy and several White House aides back to Washington from Dallas. Earlier, President John F. Kennedy had been assassinated, and the speed with which this ceremony was arranged—and the photo released—was purposeful. Johnson and his advisers wanted to assure a shocked nation that the government was stable, the situation under control. Images from the Zapruder film of the shooting, which would raise so many questions, would not be made public for days.

Photograph by **Cecil W. Stoughton**

The Beatles Arrive 1964

Two veteran photogs, Bill Eppridge and Eddie Adams, were in the throng at New York's JFK Airport, waiting for the lads to land and comparing notes on where to best position themselves. "Well," one said, "the best spot's in the plane." Finally, the plane alit, the door opened, the Beatles popped out, and there, up above, was young Scotsman Harry Benson, directing the Fabs' historic arrival on American soil. Yes, it was the music, yes, it was the hair, yes, it was Ed Sullivan. But it was also the vibrant photography, particularly Benson's, that helped create the mania, setting off a seismic shift in American culture.

Photograph by **Harry Benson**

Jackson, Mississippi 1963

Traditions, rules, laws: Like everywhere else, the American South had its own. But in most other places on May 28, 1963, the law did not exclude black people from drinking the same water, using the same seat, sleeping in the same hotel. Nor did it exclude blacks from sitting at a lunch counter, like the one at Woolworth's in downtown Jackson, Miss. The positive message that some people were able to draw from this unspeakable moment is that two white kids had the decency to help a fellow human endure the taunts of a mob.

Photograph by **Fred Blackwell** Jackson Daily News/AP

Another Landmark Image

It was the fourth school year since segregation had been outlawed by the Supreme Court. Things were not going well, and some southerners accused the national press of distorting matters. This picture, however, gave irrefutable testimony, as Elizabeth Eckford strides through a gantlet of white students, including Hazel Bryant (mouth open the widest), on her way to Little Rock's Central High.

Little Rock, Arkansas, 1957
Photograph from Bettmann/Corbis

Selma March 1965

Racial strife in the American South grew steadily hotter after school segregation was outlawed in 1954. Blacks fought for their rightful, equal status, with the lunch-counter sit-in, the Montgomery bus boycott, the Freedom Rides. To protest for voting rights throughout the South, Rev. Martin Luther King Jr. organized a nonviolent march in 1965 that was to proceed from Selma, Ala., to the state capital in Montgomery. King himself had to be in Washington, but the marchers gathered in Selma and set off on March 7. Along the way, state troopers used tear gas to drive the demonstrators into a housing project, then beat them savagely. "Bloody Sunday" shocked a nation and led to the Voting Rights Act of 1965.

Photograph by
James H. Karales

Birmingham 1963

For years, Birmingham, Ala., was considered "the South's toughest city," home to a large black population and a dominant class of whites that met in frequent, open hostility. Birmingham in 1963 had become the *cause célèbre* of the black civil rights movement as nonviolent demonstrators led by Rev. Martin Luther King Jr. repeatedly faced jail, dogs and high-velocity hoses in their tireless quest to topple segregation. This picture of people being pummeled by a liquid battering ram rallied support for the plight of the blacks.

Photograph by **Charles Moore** Black Star

Chicago Democratic Convention 1968

"The whole world is watching!" was the chant that filled the streets that August, as—not to put too fine a point on it—Mayor Richard J. Daley's police batoned the daylights out of peaceniks trying to wrest control of the streets of his city. It was not, however, only leftist intellectuals and conscientious objectors who wanted their message heard; there were many drawn to the streets by the prospect of inciting further an already inflamed police force. Americans were stunned that all this was happening in their country.

Photograph by **Perry C. Riddle** Chicago Daily News

Mexico City Olympics 1968

Sociologist Harry Edwards had been urging black athletes to boycott the Olympics to protest civil rights inequities in the U.S. The boycott didn't happen, but Edwards struck a chord with many, including San Jose State teammates Tommie Smith and John Carlos. After finishing first and third in the 200-meter sprint, they mounted the podium shoeless, wearing buttons supporting Edwards's Olympic Project for Human Rights. As the national anthem played, they held up their gloved fists. The runners were booted from the Games, but their gesture resonated. Note: Runner-up Peter Norman of Australia wore an OPHR button too.

Photograph by **John Dominis**

Another Landmark Image

Adolf Hitler fervently hoped the Berlin Olympics of 1936 would be a showcase of "Aryan supremacy." But American blacks, led by Jesse Owens, who won four gold medals, became the story of the Games. After the first day, during which the talent of the American team was evident, Hitler decided not to shake hands with medal winners. Minister of Propaganda Joseph Goebbels, while publicly insisting that German newspapers treat all visiting athletes courteously, wrote in his private diary after Day Two, "We Germans won a gold medal, the Americans three, of which two were Negroes. That is a disgrace." Right: Owens salutes his flag after winning the long jump, while second-place Luz Long salutes the Reich, as all German athletes were instructed to do.

Berlin Olympics, 1936
Photograph from AP

Woodstock 1969

They went to a psychedelic pasture (really in Bethel, N.Y., not Woodstock) to listen to their music, to be with people who dressed like them and talked like them and played like them. There was a shared bond on a cosmic scale, and their elders marveled that all these kids could be in one place for three days without violence or mayhem, despite pitifully inadequate facilities and food supplies, and despite rains that fell so long and hard they would have drowned any other party. The lesson was simple: These long-haired, antiwar bra-burners and boys with beads had created a field of dreams, and perhaps from it would rise something bright and beautiful for the future.

Photograph from AP

Altamont 1969

The crescendo of hope that came with Woodstock had its coda a mere four months later when violence and mayhem defined the Altamont Rock Festival in Livermore, Calif. The Rolling Stones, who had hired some Hell's Angels to police the concert, were in the middle of an incendiary set when the bikers began to feverishly assault a black man (who had a weapon). Mick Jagger pleaded with the Angels to stop, but they killed the man. It was a scary event, as the Stones' fierce, exotic sound conspired nightmarishly with obscene hatred, drowning out the blissful, harmonious chords of Woodstock.

Photograph from AP

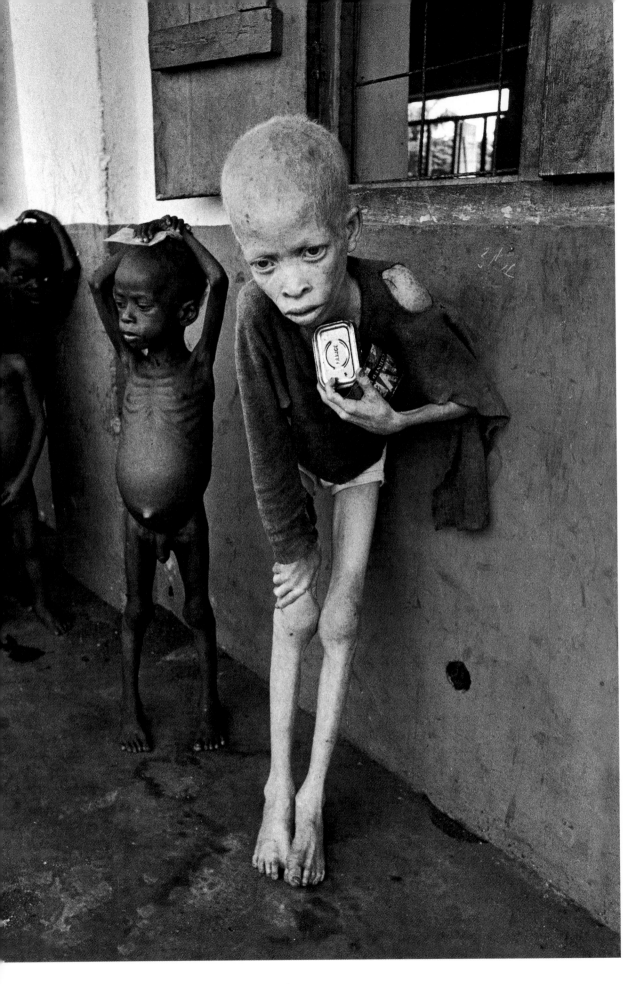

Biafra 1969

When the Igbos of eastern Nigeria declared themselves independent in 1967, Nigeria blockaded their fledgling country—Biafra. In three years of war, more than one million people died, mainly of hunger. In famine, children who lack protein often get the disease kwashiorkor, which causes their muscles to waste away and their bellies to protrude. War photographer Don McCullin drew attention to the tragedy. "I was devastated by the sight of 900 children living in one camp in utter squalor at the point of death," he said. "I lost all interest in photographing soldiers in action." The world community intervened to help Biafra, and learned key lessons about dealing with massive hunger exacerbated by war—a problem that still defies simple solutions.

Photograph by
Don McCullin
Contact Press

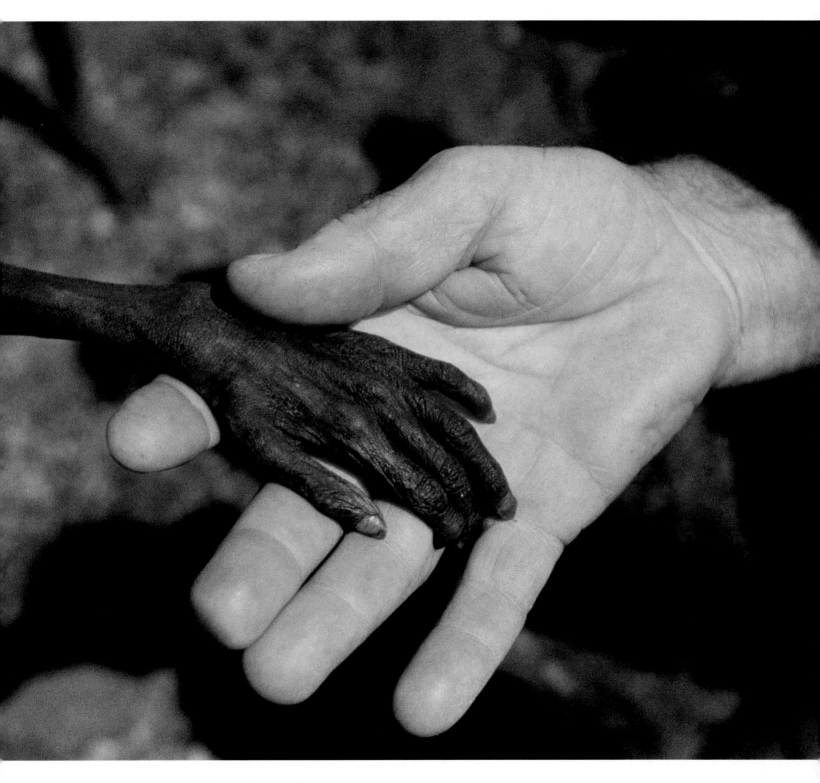

Uganda 1980

Nearly the entire Horn of Africa was parched by drought in 1980. Ethiopia, Djibouti, Eritrea, Somalia, Sudan and Uganda were all in trouble. In Uganda alone, half a million people were affected, including most newborns and many young children. Those who managed to survive barely looked human, with withered, discolored skin. They faced a life of developmental problems. Pictures like this one, of a priest holding the hand of a starving child, moved the United Nations and private groups to send food to the suffering Africans.

Photograph by **Mike Wells** Aspect Picture Library

Minamata
1971

In the 1950s and '60s, Japanese living in the coastal fishing village of Minamata complained of *itaiitabyo* ("ouch ouch disease"), which is marked by tremors and bad sight and hearing. Later the cause emerged: Chisso, a chemical company, was dumping mercury in the water. Fish and shrimp formed a large part of the local diet, and many villagers were suffering or dying. Tomoko Uemura, seen here in 1971 being bathed by her mother, was poisoned in the womb and born blind, mute and with mangled limbs. W. Eugene Smith's famous *Tomoko Uemura in Her Bath* gave a face to the effects of industrial mercury poisoning and led to the company's allocating funds for the victims.

Photograph by
W. Eugene Smith
Black Star

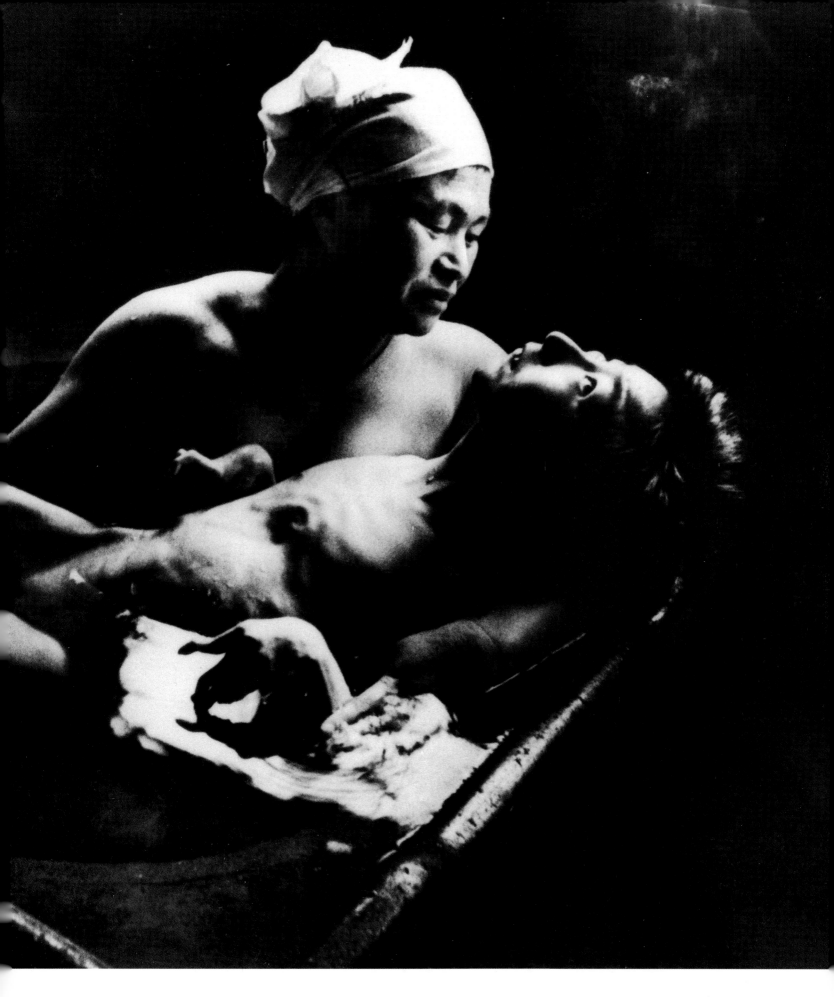

Munich Olympic Village 1972

Terrorism is always disturbing, but when it plays out in an arena whose purpose is to augment global peace, it seems yet more ghastly. The athletes from 121 nations had assembled in Munich for the 1972 Olympics when, on September 5 at 4:30 a.m., five men dressed in tracksuits toting weapons in their gym bags scaled the fence of the Olympic Village and joined up with three others already inside. They rapped on the door of the Israeli wrestling coach, shot him and a weightlifter dead, then took nine Israelis hostage. The abductors, who claimed to be from a Palestinian guerrilla group called Black September, demanded that Israel release 200 Arab prisoners. By three o'clock the next morning, after hours of tenterhook negotiations, a botched rescue attempt left the nine Israelis dead, along with five terrorists and a policeman. Three terrorists were captured. This portrait of a goon haunts anyone who remembers the scene, and, for those who were born later, displays all too well the dark hand of terrorism.

Photograph by **Kurt Strumpf** AP

Canadian Seal Hunt 1969

The annual spring seal-hunting season in far northern Canada was shown to the wider world beginning in the mid-'60s. Images such as this one from Northumberland Strait, which shows a mother seal in the background watching her offspring being killed, ran everywhere and caused a collective outrage. Many consumers stopped buying fur, and some countries banned seal-fur imports from Canada. An unintended consequence: Certain indigenous peoples, hurt by the falloff in a longtime livelihood, sold oil-drilling rights to petroleum companies in order to survive, leading to wanton environmental degradation in Canada.

Photograph by **Duncan Cameron** Capital Press

Exxon Valdez Oil Spill 1989

On March 24, the *Exxon Valdez* ran aground in Alaska's Prince William Sound, and 10.8 million gallons of crude flowed into the bay, causing the worst maritime environmental disaster in U.S. history. A quarter million seabirds, 2,800 sea otters, 300 harbor seals, 250 bald eagles and more than 20 killer whales died, and 1,300 miles of shoreline was fouled. The public outcry led to a U.S. law demanding double-hull construction in future tankers, and a jury ordered Exxon to pay billions, a verdict the company is still fighting. Meanwhile, in Alaska, more oil washes up every year.

Photograph by
John S. Lough
Department of
Environmental Conservation

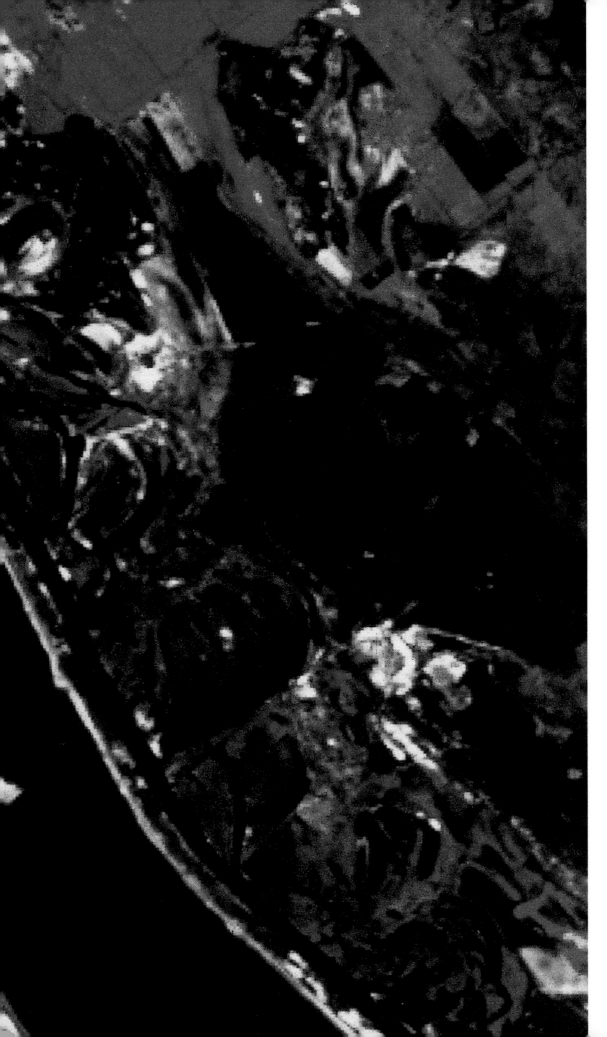

Chernobyl 1986

The Soviet Union first denied anything was wrong when Nordic countries confronted them with evidence that a radioactive cloud from there was wafting over Europe. The Soviets then admitted to a small accident at the Chernobyl nuclear plant in northern Ukraine. They said it was under control and that only two people had died. In the surrounding region, people were given little information, but American scientists, armed with satellite photos, reported that a fire was raging free. As a precaution, one European nation banned the sale of new milk, another country ordered pregnant women and young kids indoors, and handed out iodine solutions 24 hours a day. "The Soviets owe the world an explanation," President Ronald Reagan said of history's largest nuclear accident. At least 30 people died in the blast, and another 4,000 in the aftermath. The ultimate death toll remains uncertain, but is growing. Millions will be affected for decades.

Photograph from NASA

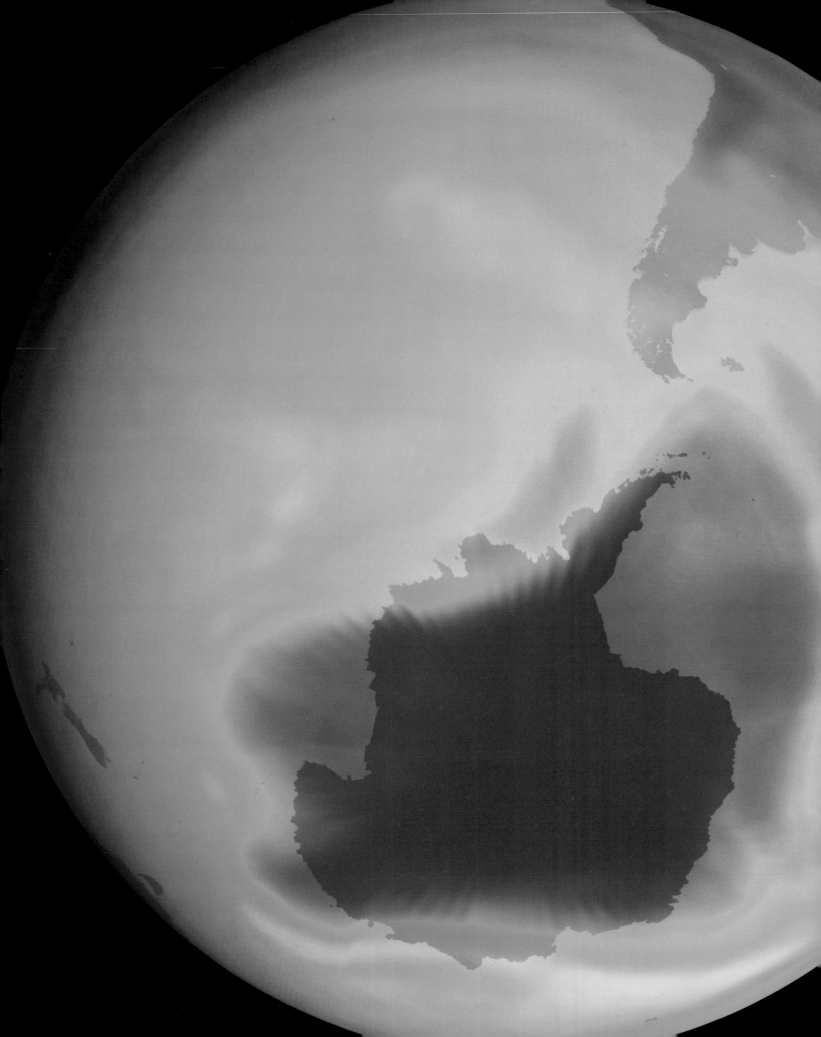

The Ozone Hole 1985

The ozone layer of Earth's atmosphere provides a sheltering veil from ultraviolet light, which causes cancer and damages essential phytoplankton. Decades ago scientists began to notice changes in the layer, then were shocked in 1985 when Joe Farman of the British Antarctic Survey found a thinning in the layer over the polar continent. The so-called ozone hole was a local springtime depletion exacerbated by such chemicals as chloroflourocarbons. Two years after Farman's find, most nations signed a pact to phase out CFCs, which may linger for a century. By 2000, the "hole" had grown to three times the size of the United States, but is now shrinking as CFC levels decline.

Photograph by **NASA GSFC** Total Ozone Mapping Spectrometer

Giant Iceberg 1995

When this photo appeared in *Time* and other influential publications, some advocates of the greenhouse theory, e.g., that industrial-waste gases are raising global temperatures, seized the moment as gargantuan evidence that the future contains the specter of serious catastrophic results, such as coastal flooding, drought and species extinction. However, scientists are far from certain that this iceberg the size of Connecticut, broken free from the Antarctic peninsula, validates any notion of global warming. Nevertheless, for those sure that global warming is nigh, the photo gave the means to an end, drawing the attention of the general public to the issue.

Photograph by **Dr. Hans Oerter** British Antarctic Survey

Milk Carton 1984

Johnny Gosch was a 12-year-old from West Des Moines who vanished while delivering papers in 1982. Juanita Estevez, 15, of Yuba City, Calif., disappeared on her way to school in 1984. These were the first two kids to be pictured on a milk carton. Child abduction was becoming a growing nightmare, and families and authorities were eager to try any method. Since then, postcards with photos of missing children have been widely distributed by mail, and have proved fruitful: One in six of the kids in these and other photo efforts are recovered. As for Juanita and Johnny: She escaped from her abductors in 1986; he is still missing.

Photograph by **Robert Frieder**

Oklahoma City 1995

One of the blackest moments in American history came when a terrorist bomb destroyed the federal building in Oklahoma City at 9:02 a.m. on April 19, 1995. Of the 168 people killed, 19 were children. That the innocent were slain by their countryman made it all the more unbearable. In this Pulitzer Prize–winning photo, firefighter Chris Fields holds one little victim, Baylee Almon, who the day before had celebrated her first birthday. The man who took the picture was a utility worker. Because he was on company time, and using a company camera, ownership was initially disputed.

Photograph by **Charles Porter IV** Zuma

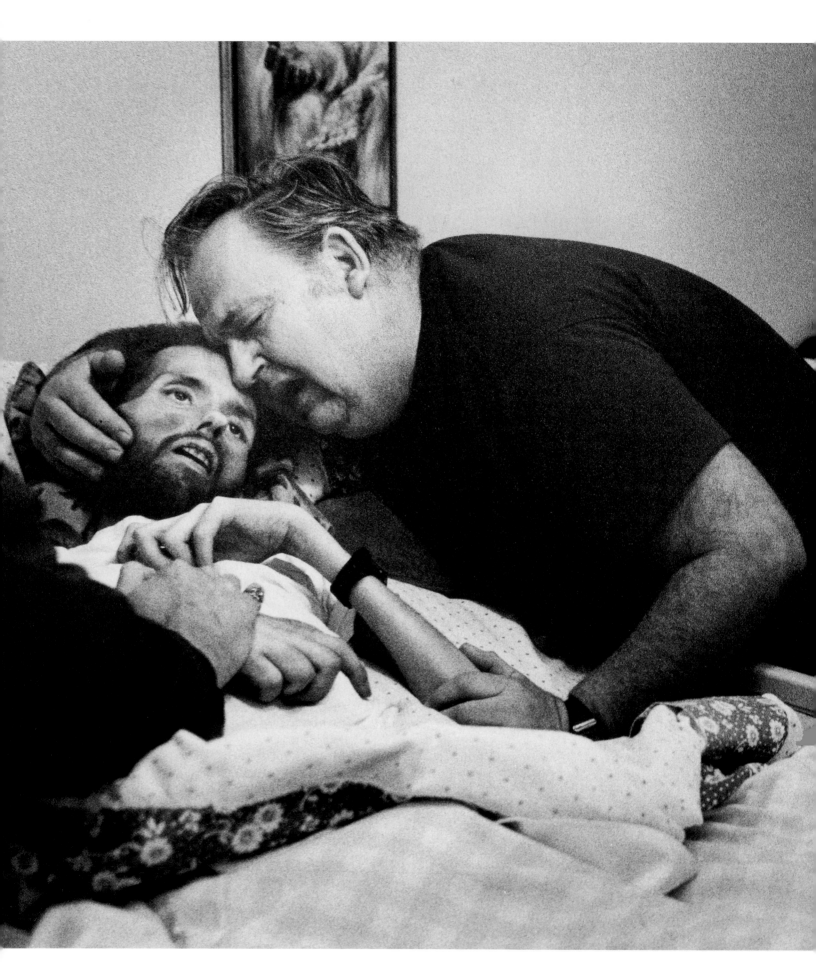

David Kirby
1990

When LIFE ran this photo of AIDS activist Kirby, visited at his deathbed by family members, the magazine was credited with destigmatizing a plague. Kirby's father, William, was impressed by the reaction to the picture—"Nobody had ever seen, publicly, how bad it was toward the end"—and the family subsequently allowed the Italian clothing company Benetton to use the image in an ad. Designer Tibor Kalman colorized Frare's photograph, and the company said the intent of its stylized presentation was to force the world to think about the epidemic. But whereas LIFE had been applauded for humanizing AIDS, Benetton was criticized in many corners for exploiting misery for commercial gain.

Photograph by
Therese Frare

Breast Cancer 1993

The artist Matuschka was diagnosed with breast cancer in 1991. Only after surgery did she learn her mastectomy was unnecessary. "So I lost a breast, and the world gained an activist," she said. This jarring self-portrait appeared on a 1993 *New York Times Magazine* cover along with the words, "You Can't Look Away Anymore." A gauntlet had been cast, and the action created precisely the desired effect. Said one advocate for the cause: "Her cover did more for Breast Cancer than anyone else in the last 25 years."

Photograph by **Matuschka**

Another Landmark Image

This is C.H. Long, a 39-year-old foreman at the JA ranch in the Texas panhandle, a place described as "320,000 acres of nothing much." Once a week, Long would ride into town for a store-bought shave and a milk shake. Maybe he'd take in a movie if a western was playing. He said things like, "If it weren't for a good horse, a woman would be the sweetest thing in the world." He rolled his own smokes. When the cowboy's face and story appeared in LIFE in 1949, advertising exec Leo Burnett had an inspiration. The company Philip Morris, which had introduced Marlboro as a woman's cigarette in 1924, was seeking a new image for the brand, and the Marlboro Man based on Long boosted Marlboro to the top of the worldwide cigarette market.

Clarence Hailey Long, 1949
Photograph by **Leonard McCombe**

Chinese Baby
1997

A group of Americans came upon this abandoned boy on a path in Fuyang and took him to a local hospital, where they were told by a staffer, "You should have left it where it was." A day later, another baby was found in the same spot, and the day after that, the first child, suffering from pneumonia and a deformed heart, died anonymously. This picture and the accompanying story caused an uproar, as human rights activists placed the blame for a plague of abandonment and infanticide squarely on the government's One Couple, One Child policy. Baby girls were at greater risk than boys, who might one day be of more use in the fields: Some estimates held that more than 1.5 million girls, out of the 13 million children born in China each year, were being abandoned. Though the government countered that parents with "feudal ideas" were causing the problem, it eventually relaxed the One Child policy—a little.

Photograph by **Jeff Abelin**

Elsie Wright

Frances Griffiths with Fairies c. 1916

Two young girls in the village of Cottingly borrowed a camera and took a few photos that tapped directly into English society's borderline-perverse fascination with fairies. Sir Arthur Conan Doyle certified the pictures' authenticity: "Matter as we have known it is not really the limit of our universe." In 1983 the naughty Elsie finally fessed up: The fairies were cutouts.

Trick Photography

If these were real photographs of real things, they would certainly have changed the world. As it is, they are either exposed or yet-to-be-exposed pictures of the supernatural. They are hoaxes and jokes, and they have been part of the easily manipulated medium of photography since the beginning. Some of these images have attracted legions of believers, and in this they have changed the world, making it a far more spiritual place.

BBC Publications

Photographer Unknown
Young Girl with Ghost c. 1860

Ghosts have a long tradition of popping into pictures, and spooky photos were all the rage during the late-1800s age of spiritualism.

Christian Spurling

The Loch Ness Monster **1934**

The *London Daily Mail* hired big-game hunter M.A. Wetherell to shoot the storied Nessie—on film. All he found in Scotland were some prankster's fake footprints, but he subsequently conspired with modelmaker Spurling to customize a monster out of a toy sub, then floated this famous image.

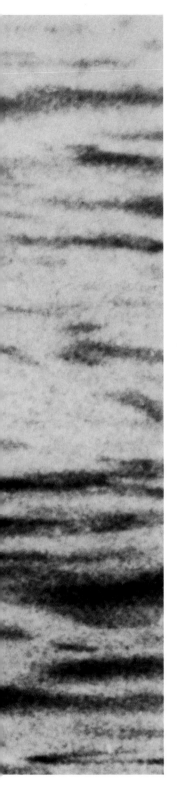

Ralph Ditter
Unidentified Flying Object 1967

It's a bird! It's a plane! It's a . . . flying saucer?!? Ditter, a Zanesville, Ohio, barber, said he took this picture from his home. UFOs are prime candidates for camera tricksters. Or are they?

Roger Patterson
Bigfoot 1967

A.k.a. Sasquatch, a big, hirsute creature, part human, part God-knows-what, that roams the forests of the Pacific Northwest. Except that when Ray Wallace died in 2002, his family admitted that he had started the hoax in 1958 with fake footprints, and, later, a Bigfoot suit.

War & Peace

The Crimean War 1855

A British solicitor with an artistic bent, Roger Fenton took up the paintbrush and then, after seeing photography on display at the Great Exhibition in Hyde Park in 1851, the camera. Fenton shot landscapes and portraits, and pictures of Queen Victoria's children at Windsor Castle in 1854. The next year, he was assigned by a print dealer to cover the Crimean War, being waged by England and France against Russia. Thus the war became the first conflict with any substantial photographic record. Battling cholera and broken ribs, lugging his developing lab on a horse-drawn carriage, Fenton produced 350 images. They are stately and sedate for war photography, since neither the queen nor Fenton's sponsors wanted to see carnage or any evidence of a war that was progressing badly.

Photograph by
Roger Fenton

Gettysburg
1863

Photographer Gardner worked for the renowned Mathew Brady, whose firm had been granted access to Civil War battlefields by the Union. Gardner wrote that photographs of dead soldiers meant to convey to the viewer "the blank horror and reality of war, in opposition to its pageantry . . . Here are the dreadful details! Let them aid in preventing another such calamity falling upon the nation." His images certainly conveyed horror and therefore had an astonishing impact on the public consciousness, but the pictures' relationship to reality was strained. In *The Home of a Rebel Sharpshooter, Gettysburg,* for instance, the dead Confederate soldier has been moved to his resting place in Devil's Den from elsewhere on the battlefield, and a rifle has been positioned just so to create a perfect composition.

Photograph by **Alexander Gardner**
National Archives

Hitler 1934

No other person in the 20th century so realized and successfully employed propaganda as Adolf Hitler. His rise to power and explosive, horrific tenure were awash in psychological flummery, potent imagery and hypnotic oratory. For a country crushed less than two decades earlier in a world war, for a hungry, once proud people, the avatar had come . . . and here, with intensity already flooding his countenance, he rises toward the podium to deliver a speech at Bückeburg. This image could, and would, kill.

Photograph by **Heinrich Hoffmann**

Another Landmark Image

Mao Zedong had for some time let others run the Chinese Communist Party when, in 1966, he decided to retake the reins. To show that he was physically strong, he and a few of his cronies swam in the Yangtze River, all the while exchanging jokes with the gathered masses. The Chinese media, of course, took all this in thirstily, and Mao scored a major victory that helped him kick off his Cultural Revolution.

The Yangtze River, 1966
Photograph from Bettmann/Corbis

Shanghai Bombed
1937

Japan launched its bid to annex China in July 1937, following years of planning. The bombing of Shanghai on August 14, "Bloody Saturday," was appalling in the price paid by helpless civilians. The photo of this child deserted at the train station jarred its beholders, and with the Rape of Nanking four months later—a barbaric massacre of as many as 300,000 Chinese—the image of the quiet, tea-drinking Japanese was forever altered. It was later learned that the photographer may have staged the train station picture, but the damage, in every sense, had been done. This early awareness of Japanese war atrocities helped fuel the subsequent American revulsion at—and response to—the attack on Pearl Harbor.

Photograph by **H. S. Wong**
National Archives

The Falling Soldier
1936

It is perhaps the most famous war photograph of all time and it is certainly one of the most controversial. *Loyalist Militiaman at the Moment of Death, Cerro Muriano, September 5, 1936* is either a shockingly intimate depiction of a Spanish Republican soldier breathing his last during his country's civil war, as LIFE believed in '37 and most observers still maintain, or it is staged, as a British historian first argued in 1975. Either way, the image has long had a massive impact. In his 2002 biography of the storied Capa, Alex Kershaw wrote that the "truth" of the photo resides in its presentation of death: "The Falling Soldier, authentic or fake, is ultimately a record of Capa's political bias and idealism . . . Indeed, he would soon come to experience the brutalizing insanity and death of illusions that all witnesses who get close enough to the 'romance' of war inevitably confront."

Photograph by
Robert Capa Magnum

Saint Paul's During the Blitz 1940

The German Luftwaffe began a withering campaign against Great Britain in July 1940. Initially designed as a preinvasion attack, the shelling focused on London and other cities in September. From the seventh day of that month, the capital city was bombed 57 nights in a row; in all, some 10,000 Londoners were killed. Saint Paul's was designed by Christopher Wren and built hundreds of years earlier. This image of the ancient cathedral surviving in the midst of mayhem gave solace, and strength, to a weary people.

Photograph by **John Topham** International News Photos/Corbis

Another Landmark Image

The Blitz had brought pain and destruction to the East End of London, home to industry and poor folk. Queen Elizabeth and King George VI lived in Buckingham Palace, in the West End. Before September 13, 1940, the palace had been unscathed, but that night bombs fell within the grounds (here the royal couple, at left, inspect the ruins). Aligning herself squarely with her struggling subjects, Elizabeth said, "Now we can look the East End in the face."

Buckingham Palace, 1940
Photograph from AP

Dead on the Beach 1943

When LIFE ran this stark, haunting photograph of a beach in Papua New Guinea on September 20, 1943, the magazine felt compelled to ask in an adjacent full-page editorial, "Why print this picture, anyway, of three American boys dead upon an alien shore?" Among the reasons: "words are never enough . . . words do not exist to make us see, or know, or feel what it is like, what actually happens." But there was more to it than that; LIFE was actually publishing in concert with government wishes. President Franklin D. Roosevelt was convinced that Americans had grown too complacent about the war, so he lifted the ban on images depicting U.S. casualties. Strock's picture and others that followed in LIFE and elsewhere had the desired effect. The public, shocked by combat's grim realities, was instilled with yet greater resolve to win the war.

Photograph by **George Strock**

Another Landmark Image

Robert Capa, who once famously observed that "If your pictures aren't good enough, you're not close enough," was on the shore with the first wave on D-Day, working for LIFE. He shot four rolls of soldiers slogging onto Omaha Beach, storming the cliffs, hunkering down. Then, a photo assistant in London ruined all but a dozen images. Their grainy, shell-shocked feel defined the tension and texture of the Longest Day. Years later, they informed the look of Steven Spielberg's *Saving Private Ryan*.

Omaha Beach, D-Day, 1944
Photograph by **Robert Capa** Magnum

Saipan 1944

When Japan threw its best punch on December 7, 1941, the United States knew it was in for a hell of a time in the Pacific. That turned out to be all too true. The Navy struck back quickly at Midway, and the long island-hopping campaign had begun: Americans had to go in on the ground and fight to the death with defenders who had been preparing for years. But, despite all the bloodshed, despite the many atrocities, one look at this Marine on Saipan told the folks back home, "It's tough, but we're gonna lick them!"

Photograph by **W. Eugene Smith**

Yalta 1945

The leaders of the main Allied powers met at Yalta on the Crimean Peninsula in February to hash out two matters: how to engineer Germany's final defeat, and, perhaps more pressing at this stage, how to occupy the defeated land. So, in this picture, there are two wars afoot, and each man already has his game face on for the next one. If Churchill, Roosevelt and Stalin evinced togetherness, it was strictly for the camera and for the Allied peoples. They were, of course, photographed sitting down because of FDR's polio.

Photograph from U.S. Army Signal Corps

Benito Mussolini

1945

He was the man who made the trains run on time, but over time, he wore out his welcome. One of the most charismatic leaders of the century, he rose from rather humble beginnings to become in 1922 the youngest prime minister (he was 39) in Italian history. Hitler quite admired him but proved his undoing when Il Duce saw the spoils accruing to Hitler and caught the fever: In 1940 he dragged his totally unprepared nation into WWII. Fascism would become a dirty word in Italy, and the man who sought to be the next Caesar was caught trying to flee the country in a German greatcoat. He, his mistress Claretta Petacci and others were shot dead and hanged from the heels in Milan's Piazza Loreto. A radio broadcast from the scene: "It is interesting to see the hate, the fury . . . They want the bodies to stay there for six months . . . This is a good example."

Photograph by
12th Combat Camera Crew

Another Landmark Image

For a quarter century, Nicolae Ceausescu ran Romania with secret police, Mao-like economic plans, and a cult of personality. His downfall was as brutal and bizarre as his regime. Generals called in to quash a protest switched sides, and Ceausescu then called a rally of 100,000, which turned on him. He and his wife fled in a helicopter, were apprehended, tried and then executed on Christmas Day, 1989. Confusion and violence reigned until the bodies were displayed.

Nicolae Ceausescu, 1989
Photograph by **Christopher Pillitz** Hulton Archive/Getty

Anne Frank 1941

Six million Jews died in the Holocaust. For many throughout the world, one teenage girl gave them a story and a face. She was Anne Frank, the adolescent who, according to her diary, retained her hope and humanity as she hid with her family in an Amsterdam attic. In 1944 the Nazis, acting on a tip, arrested the Franks; Anne and her sister died of typhus at Bergen-Belsen only a month before the camp was liberated. The world came to know her through her words and through this ordinary portrait of a girl of 14. She stares with big eyes, wearing an enigmatic expression, gazing at a future that the viewer knows will never come.

Photographer Unknown

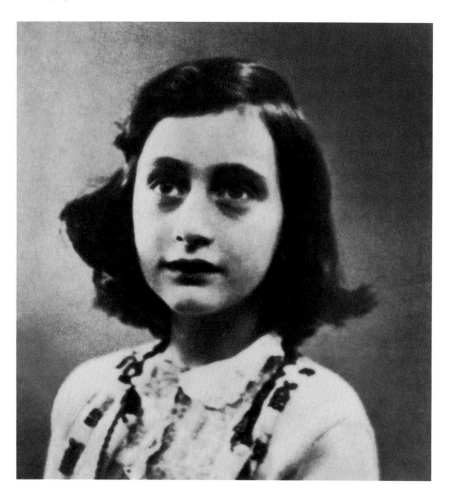

Buchenwald 1945

LIFE photographer Margaret Bourke-White was with Gen. George Patton's troops when they liberated the Buchenwald concentration camp. Forty-three thousand people had been murdered there. Patton was so outraged he ordered his men to march German civilians through the camp so they could see with their own eyes what their nation had wrought. Bourke-White's pictures carried the horrible images to the world. In America the pictures proved that reports of the Nazi's methodical extermination of the Jews were true, and the country began a long process of rethinking its behavior, such as the decision not to bomb the camps.

Photograph by **Margaret Bourke-White**

Prisoners' Hand Marks 1944

The camera is a masterly tool for documenting some of the vilest of incidents, ones where words fail. This photograph was taken after the German occupation of France during World War II. It depicts the wall of a torture chamber on the Boulevard Victor in Paris. The desperate hands of prisoners have inflicted themselves into the asbestos as the effects of electrical current became more than they could bear. Such happenings may be forgiven but cannot be forgotten, not with this document. The Parisian Roger Schall had been allowed by the Nazis to photograph life there during the war, but with the liberation, he took very different kinds of pictures—like this one—and his work was used in postwar prosecutions. Schall's brother published a book of such pictures at war's end, and it became a mandatory buy in Paris.

Photograph by **Roger Schall**

Another Landmark Image

French soldiers and civilians are being processed at the border of the American and Soviet occupation zones for their return home when, suddenly, one woman denounces another as a Gestapo stool pigeon. Vengeance was primal. It was also tribunal: At the first international war-crimes trial in Nuremberg, Germany, 11 Nazis were sentenced to death, seven sent to jail and three acquitted.

Vengeance in Dessau, 1945
Photograph by **Henri Cartier-Bresson** Magnum

Iwo Jima 1945

U.S. Marines raised the flag atop Iwo Jima's Mount Suribachi on February 23, 1945, and AP photographer Rosenthal made one of the most iconic pictures ever. (Another shot of the same incident taken from a different angle by a Marine photographer is not as compelling, nor as famous, but proves beyond doubt that Rosenthal's shot was not staged.) The photo, which showed emphatically just who was on the ascent in the Pacific theater, had a pure, inspirational quality. In the States, work began instantly on a statue based upon this tableau.

Photograph by **Joe Rosenthal** AP

MacArthur Returns 1945

When Japan attacked Pearl Harbor in 1941, it also invaded the Philippines, where Gen. Douglas MacArthur was based. It was surely painful for this most zealous of soldiers when President Roosevelt ordered him to evacuate to Australia. When he arrived in Adelaide, MacArthur said to reporters, "I shall return." In October 1944, he did so, to great fanfare. The image that remains indelible, however, was actually taken three months later when his old friend Carl Mydans recorded his arrival at another beachhead, in Luzon. MacArthur, of course, preferred the grander image—as did the world at large.

Photograph by **Carl Mydans**

Nagasaki 1945

Nothing like the mushroom cloud had ever been seen, not by the general public. It was a suitably awesome image for the power unleashed below. On August 6 the first atomic bomb killed an estimated 80,000 people in the Japanese city of Hiroshima. There was no quick surrender, and three days later a second bomb exploded 500 meters above the ground in Nagasaki. The blast wind, heat rays reaching several thousand degrees and radiation destroyed anything even remotely nearby, killing or injuring as many as 150,000 at the time, and more later. As opposed to the very personal images of war that had brought the pain home, the ones from Japan that were most shocking were those from a longer perspective, showing the enormity of what had occurred.

Photograph from U.S. Air Force

Another Landmark Image

Americans—and everyone—had heard of the bomb that "leveled" Hiroshima, but what did that mean? When the aerial photography was published, that question was answered. For many, the promise of an end to the war overwhelmed considerations about tomorrow. But, slowly, the devastation of Hiroshima and Nagasaki sank in, and a thought emerged: We can blow up the world.

Hiroshima, Three Weeks After the Bomb, 1945
Photograph by **George Silk**

U-2 1960

At first, the United States did not admit to spying on the U.S.S.R., despite the fact that the Soviets said they had shot down a U-2, which was an American spy plane. But the evidence in this photo of captured pilot Francis Gary Powers finally forced President Dwight D. Eisenhower to acknowledge—and suspend—the program. The incident made the cold war colder: A summit meeting collapsed after Ike refused to apologize. Powers was sentenced to 10 years, but was brought home after nearly two years in a dramatic exchange for a Soviet spy on a Berlin bridge.

Photograph by
Carl Mydans

Cuban Missile Crisis 1962

On October 22, 1962, after accusing the U.S.S.R. of installing nuclear missiles on Cuba, President John F. Kennedy ordered a blockade of the island. When the Soviet ambassador to the U.N. refused to deny the charge, U.S. ambassador Adlai Stevenson confronted him with these photos of missile sites taken by the high-flying spy plane, the U-2, and the Soviets were compelled to back down. The presentation of seemingly incontrovertible evidence would become known as an "Adlai Stevenson moment." Robert F. Kennedy later admitted that he and his brother found the grainy images quite baffling, and banked on the interpretation proffered by the CIA: "I, for one, had to take their word for it."

Photograph by **Neal Boenzi** The New York Times/Redux

South of the DMZ 1966

Contrary to the constraints that were put upon the press in subsequent conflicts, and even to the embedded program used in the recent Iraqi war, correspondents and photographers in Vietnam could, as Walter Cronkite wrote in LIFE, "accompany troops to wherever they could hitch a ride, and there was no censorship . . . That system—or lack of one—kept the American public well informed of our soldiers' problems, their setbacks and their heroism." *Reaching Out* is a quintessential example of the powerful imagery that came out of Vietnam. "The color photographs of tormented Vietnamese villagers and wounded American conscripts that Larry Burrows took and LIFE published, starting in 1962, certainly fortified the outcry against the American presence in Vietnam," Susan Sontag wrote in her essay "Looking at War," in the December 9, 2002, *New Yorker.* "Burrows was the first important photographer to do a whole war in color—another gain in verisimilitude and shock." Burrows was killed when the helicopter he was riding in was shot down over Laos in 1971.

Photograph by
Larry Burrows

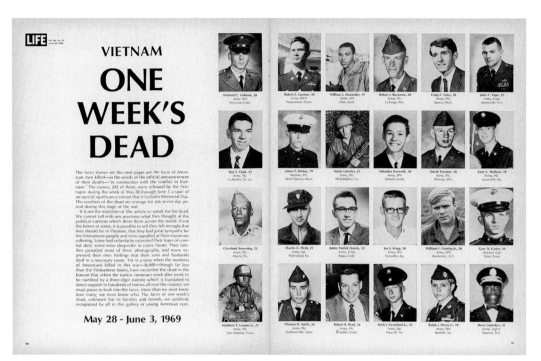

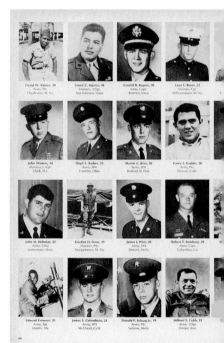

One Week's Dead   May 28–June 3, 1969

By 1969, Americans were dying in Vietnam each week by the hundreds. Total losses had reached a staggering 36,000. To personalize the figures, LIFE ran the name, hometown and picture of each serviceman whom the Pentagon said was killed during the Memorial Day week. Their families sent most of the photos, usually the timeless military portrait. But then, Patrick Hagerty, 19, of Youngstown, Ohio, was climbing a pole and Johnnie Brigman, 23, of North, S.C., was suavely posing by a car. Some families said the war was just; others said their sons had been desperate to come home. LIFE, over 12 pages that became part of the national conversation, just wanted Americans to know their 242 countrymen: "When the nation continues week after week to be numbed by a three-digit statistic, which is translated to direct anguish in hundreds of homes all over the country, we must pause to look into the faces . . . the faces of one week's dead."

LIFE June 27, 1969

My Lai 1968

A company commander told his forces that My Lai was a Viet Cong stronghold. Encountering little if any resistance, they destroyed the village anyway. Some 500 civilians were killed, huts burned, livestock slaughtered and a well poisoned with a corpse. However, the Army treated My Lai as routine combat until the truth came out the following fall. LIFE ran Army photographer Ron Haeberle's documentation of the massacre, including this shot of a mother sheltering her 13-year-old daughter from molestation by GIs, just moments before both were slain. The savagery nauseated Americans, turning them further against the war.

Photograph by **Ronald S. Haeberle**

Kent State 1970

When President Richard Nixon said he was sending troops to Cambodia, the nation's colleges erupted in protest. At Kent State some threw rocks. The Ohio National Guard, called in to quell the turmoil, suddenly turned and fired, killing four; two were simply walking to class. This photo captured a pivotal moment: American soldiers had just killed American kids. Student photographer John Filo won the Pulitzer; the event was also memorialized in a Neil Young song and a TV movie. The girl, Mary Ann Vecchio, turned out not to be a Kent State student, but a 14-year-old runaway. She was sent back to her family in Florida.

Photograph by **John Paul Filo** Valley Daily News/AP

Execution of a Viet Cong Guerrilla 1968

With North Vietnam's Tet Offensive beginning, Nguyen Ngoc Loan, South Vietnam's national police chief, was doing all he could to keep Viet Cong guerrillas from Saigon. As Loan executed a prisoner who was said to be a Viet Cong captain, AP photographer Eddie Adams opened the shutter. Adams won a Pulitzer Prize for a picture that, as much as any, turned public opinion against the war. Adams felt that many misinterpreted the scene, and when told in 1998 that the immigrant Loan had died of cancer at his home in Burke, Va., he said, "The guy was a hero. America should be crying. I just hate to see him go this way, without people knowing anything about him."

Photograph by **Eddie Adams** AP

Napalm Strike 1972

Another complicated image showed South Vietnamese children burned by napalm, which had accidentally been dropped by South Vietnamese planes. The details notwithstanding, the photograph horrified. After taking it, Nick Ut, who was born in South Vietnam, doused the naked Kim Phuc with water and rushed her to a hospital. Phuc, who lives in Toronto, credits Ut with saving her life. The picture won a Pulitzer, and after the war, Ut moved to AP's Los Angeles bureau. In 2002, tapes were released that had President Nixon wondering to H.R. Haldeman about whether the "napalm thing . . . was a fix."

Photograph by **Nick Ut** AP

Vietnam 1975

President Richard Nixon talked of getting out of Vietnam, but carefully used the phrase "peace with honor." By April 1975, however, it was apparent that South Vietnam was about to fall, and emergency evacuation plans were put into action. Dignity was scrapped as Americans (and a small number of South Vietnamese) fought to get aboard the last transit out. Here, U.S. pilot Robert Hedrix punches a South Vietnamese army deserter trying to force his way onto a DC-6 departing Nha Trang. In the U.S., images such as these said: America, previously invincible, has lost a war and is sneaking out of town.

Photograph by **Thai Khac Chuong** Bettmann/Corbis

Cambodia 1979

The world did not know the extent of the genocide that dictator Pol Pot had heaped on Cambodia until it was overrun by Vietnam. Then, in 1979, mass graves and fastidiously stacked skulls were discovered. Some four years earlier, Pot's Khmer Rouge had taken power partly on anti-U.S. sentiment generated by American air strikes there from 1969 to '73. But it was becoming obvious that Pot had executed the educated and built an economy out of agrarian slave labor, sending a peaceful and civilized country back to the stone age. Perhaps a quarter of Cambodia's population was dead, either from execution or starvation.

Photograph by **Jay Ullal** Stern/Black Star

Nixon in China 1972

It was the most populous nation on the planet, one very far from the United States both in distance and in philosophy. Richard Nixon had fashioned a political career out of being a hard-liner on communism, but he also was respected, even by his critics, as a top-drawer student of international affairs. So there was a certain irony, if not surprise, when he was all smiles with Mao Zedong at the beginning of his historic 1972 visit to China. Nixon had put an end to decades of silence between the two nations.

Photograph from AP

Peace Treaty 1979

For many years, peace in the Middle East had seemed unattainable. Jews claimed a right to Israel by history, the Bible and the U.N.; surrounding and displaced Arabs vowed to push the new country into the sea. Then, in 1979, President Jimmy Carter managed to wrangle Israeli Prime Minister Menachem Begin and Egyptian President Anwar Sadat into a handshake and a deal. Israel would give up the Sinai Peninsula, occupied in 1967's Six-Day War, and Egypt would become the first Arab state to recognize Israel. The accord also gave Palestinians some self-determination. Still, the Arab world was furious and this famous handshake cost Sadat his life: He was assassinated in 1981.

Photograph by **Bob Daugherty** AP

Other Landmark Images

Facing a gun down may be the ultimate act of civil disobedience. In 1967, hundreds of thousands of protesters gathered in Washington, D.C., to express their views on the war in Vietnam. Phil Strang from the University of Illinois strode up to National Guardsmen for this memorable scene. The next year, a worker in Bratislava bared his chest before a Soviet tank after Moscow decided to put a lid on Alexander Dubcek's attempt in Czechoslovakia to make communism a less totalitarian state.

**Vietnam War
Protest, 1967**
Photograph by
Bernie Boston

**Bratislava,
1968**
Photograph
from Stern

Tiananmen Square 1989

A hunger strike by 3,000 students in Beijing had grown to a protest of more than a million as the injustices of a nation cried for reform. For seven weeks the people and the People's Republic, in the person of soldiers dispatched by a riven Communist Party, warily eyed each other as the world waited. When this young man simply would not move, standing with his meager bags before a line of tanks, a hero was born. A second hero emerged as the tank driver refused to crush the man, and instead drove his killing machine around him. Soon this dream would end, and blood would fill Tiananmen. But this picture had shown a billion Chinese that there is hope.

Photograph by **Stuart Franklin** Magnum

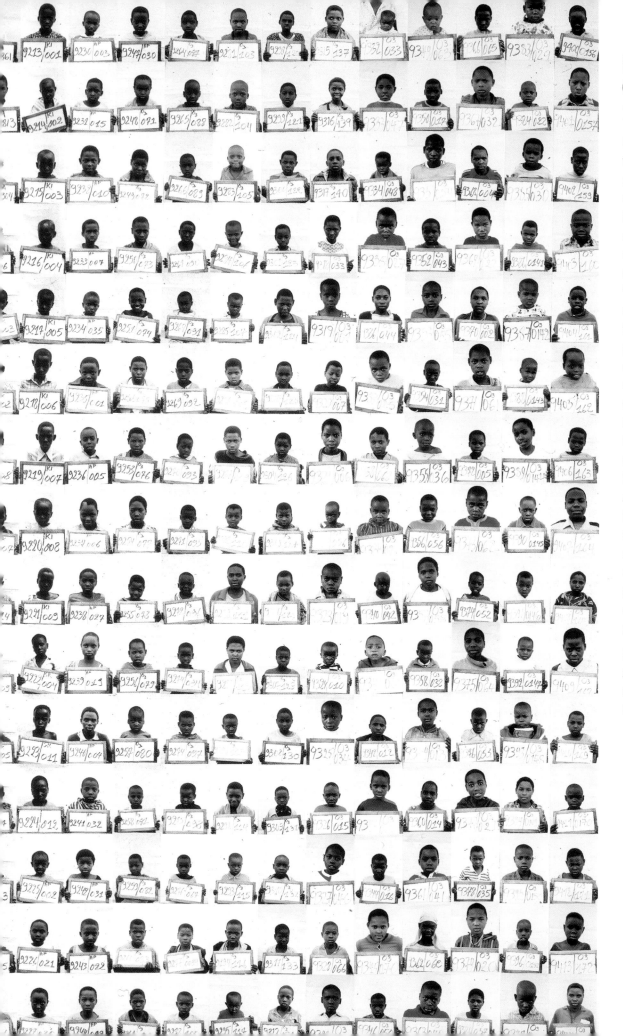

Seamus Conlan went to Rwanda as a photojournalist to cover a war—the ethnic battle between Hutu and Tutsi—and was moved by the hundreds of thousands of "unaccompanied" children who had lost their parents—either permanently to death or temporarily in the chaos. Conlan gave each child a number, sorted 21,000 of them by region and displayed their pictures in refugee camps. Although many of the kids remained orphaned, thousands of families were reunited, and aid groups have now adopted Conlan's photo system.

Photograph by
**Seamus Conlan
& Tara Farrell**
WorldPictureNews

September 11, 2001

There are memorable images of Old Glory from the Revolutionary War, the Civil War, World War II. On this day we found ourselves in yet another war, this time against terrorism. Much of the attack is familiar from oft-seen TV footage, but this photo has come to represent our ensuing pride of place. The flag then embarked on a mysterious journey. It flew from the USS *Theodore Roosevelt* near Afghanistan and was later given to New York, but at some point (perhaps in the confusion at Ground Zero) the flag had been replaced by a larger one.

Photograph by **Thomas E. Franklin** The Record

Saddam Toppled, 2003
Photograph by **Goran Tomasevic**
Reuters/Landov

Abu Ghraib, 2004

Other Landmark Images

The toppling of a 40-foot-high Saddam Hussein Statue in Baghdad's Firdos Square on April 9, 2003, was said by some to be little more than a photo op. But these events have impact. The world saw, emphatically, that a tyrant's reign was at an end. The Arab world, much of which had swallowed Iraq's account of the war's progress, saw a graphic, shocking display of American might. Of course one year later, photos emerged from the Abu Ghraib prison, also known as the Baghdad Correctional Facility, indicating that American guards and service members were engaged in the systematic abuse and even torture of prisoners of war. This image, in which a hooded Iraqi is made to stand on a box and is told that if he steps down he will be electrocuted, appeared on posters and murals throughout the Middle East, fomenting anti-U.S. rage. The pictures from Abu Ghraib not only changed the world there, but back home, where incredulous legislators and citizens on both sides of the aisle were appalled at a level of barbarity they had ascribed, only yesterday, to our enemies.

Stop Action

By this point in *100 Photographs That Changed the World,* at least some readers may be asking, "What about the Kennedy assassination?" "Where are the Twin Towers?" Those images, which are seared into our collective memory, were excerpts from film or video footage. In the modern era, selected moments "grabbed" from moving pictures can often provide the power that is commonly the province of still photography.

Paul Schutzer

Ben Martin

ABC, CBS, NBC
Televised Presidential Debate 1960

Candidates John F. Kennedy and Richard M. Nixon debated four times, and many who were listening on the radio felt Nixon won, while TV viewers saw the smooth, telegenic JFK far outshine the shady Nixon.

Zapruder Film 1967, The Sixth Floor

Abraham Zapruder
Dallas **1963**

As President John F. Kennedy's motorcade turned onto Elm Street, Zapruder trained his Bell & Howell Zoomatic on the limo. LIFE bought the rights to print frames from the film, and conspiracy theorists everywhere were able to join the FBI, Secret Service and Warren Commission in studying the Zapruder film in an attempt to learn if there had been more than one shooter.

Hibernia Bank
Patty Hearst
1974

On April 15, five robbers entered a San Francisco bank, wounded two bystanders and escaped with more than $10,000. Police were stunned to learn from the videotape that one suspect was Patty Hearst, the granddaughter of publishing tycoon William Randolph Hearst. She had been kidnapped two months earlier by a group called the Symbionese Liberation Army. She later claimed to have been brainwashed, but was convicted and sentenced to seven years.

KTLA TV

AM 12:53:30

George Holliday

L.A. Police Beating Rodney King 1991

After a car chase, the police inflicted a feral beating on King. The footage from amateur photographer Holliday startled and worried a nation already weary of police brutality. Despite the video, a jury acquitted the four police officers.

Jules Naudet, Goldfish Pictures

The First Plane Hits the World Trade Center 2001

The world is about to change, as of 8:46 a.m. on September 11, 2001: American Airlines Flight 11, laden with 20,000 gallons of jet fuel, has crashed into the World Trade Center. The French filmmaking brothers Jules and Gedeon were there to record it.

Science & Nature

Galloping Horse 1878

Was there a moment midstride when horses had all hooves off the ground? Leland Stanford, the railroad baron and future university founder, bet there was—or at least that's the story. It was 1872 when Stanford hired noted landscape photographer Eadweard Muybridge to figure it out. It took years, but Muybridge delivered: He rigged a racetrack with a dozen strings that triggered 12 cameras. Muybridge not only proved Stanford right but also set off the revolution in motion photography that would become movies. Biographer Rebecca Solnit summed up his life: "He is the man who split the second, as dramatic and far-reaching an action as the splitting of the atom."

Photographs by **Eadweard Muybridge**

Another Landmark Image

Camera shutters and film can move only so fast; the world moves faster. To capture on film what happens inside a machine, M.I.T. engineering professor Harold Edgerton developed the technique of strobe photography. His fascinating pictures found their way into art museums, but Edgerton's discoveries also had practical implications for those who studied ballistics, biomechanics and fluid dynamics.

Milkdrop Coronet, 1931
Photograph by **Harold Edgerton** ©Harold & Esther Edgerton Foundation, 2003, courtesy Palm Press, Inc.

Boston from a Captive Balloon 1860

Nadar, the pioneering French celebrity photographer, was a pioneering aerial photographer as well. But the few fruits of his earliest experiments from a balloon, undertaken in 1858, are lost, and he didn't return to the air until 1868 when he took scenics of Paris from on high. Meanwhile, in the United States, James Wallace Black, a painter-turned-photographer, employed an interesting method to give his viewers a fresh perspective of their world. He used kites and small balloons to carry his camera as high as 1,200 feet, then opened the shutter from the ground with a thin rope.

Photograph by **James Wallace Black** Gilman Paper Company Collection

Another Landmark Image

Aerial reconnaissance photographs were taken from balloons during the American Civil War, but it wasn't until Wilbur Wright shot pictures from a plane in 1909 that the military realized just how valuable scouting from the air might prove. In World War I, reconnaissance missions were the "eyes of the army" from the get-go, as two-seater planes carrying a pilot and an observer flew over enemy lines to report on positions. In 1918, French aerial units were producing as many as 10,000 photographs a day.

German Trenches near Reims, France, 1914
Photograph from the Museum of Modern Art

Chicago Fire 1871

The summer had been bone-dry, and on the evening of October 8, wind whipped wildly through the Windy City. Whether Mrs. O'Leary's cow kicked the lantern, or a visitor dropped his pipe, or a cinder from a neighbor's chimney landed on the roof, the barn belonging to Pat and Catherine O'Leary of 137 De Koven Street was soon engulfed, and when gusts blew the flames northward, so was much of Chicago. A third of the city was lost, including the downtown area; more than 200 were killed. Urban scientists began to rethink their largely wooden infrastructures, and the notion of charity drives for the victims of disaster took hold.

Photograph from Corbis

San Francisco Earthquake 1906

A little after five a.m. on April 18, 1906, a giant earthquake rocked the city of San Francisco. Felt from Oregon to southern California, the quake ruptured some 270 miles of the San Andreas fault. The epicenter was near San Francisco, severing gas mains, snapping electrical wires and setting fires throughout the city. Jack London, 40 miles away, described a "lurid tower" of fire; by the time he got there, the scene convinced him that the city was "gone." These folks on Russian Hill seem to be taking the event a bit less dramatically. In any case, 3,000 people were killed and 200,000 left homeless. Important lessons in building construction were learned from the disaster.

Photograph by
Arnold Genthe
Fine Arts Museum
of San Francisco

Old Faithful
c. 1871

In 1870, Henry Dana Washburn, a former general in the Union Army, led an expedition to find the headwaters of the Yellowstone River. He and his men were so impressed by the lakes, valleys and particularly the geysers in the region that they began lobbying Congress to preserve the wondrous land straddling the Wyoming and Montana territories as a park. Washburn's reports interested Washington, but it wasn't until legislators received portfolios of William Henry Jackson's photographs of the strange, exciting land that acclamation was general: This place must be protected. In 1872, Yellowstone became the first national park anywhere in the world. Today more than 100 countries have national parks or reserves, and the U.S. National Park Service has nearly 400 holdings.

Photograph by
William Henry Jackson
Daniel Wolf Inc.

Another Landmark Image

The titanic nature photographer Ansel Adams was a crusader with his camera every bit as much as Rachel Carson was with her pen. While he used subtle persuasion on the general public with his images, he had blunt words for bureaucrats and politicians; he once told President Gerald R. Ford, "What we need is women's liberation intensity as far as preservations of our parks is concerned."

Half Dome, Yosemite, 1960
Photograph by **Ansel Adams** Ansel Adams Trust/Corbis

Everest
1953

A Himalayan peak of 29,035 feet, the world's highest, had resisted conquest for decades. Some thought the task impossible, but when New Zealand beekeeper Edmund Hillary and Sherpa Tenzing Norgay, both climbing as part of a British expedition, reached the top on May 29, 1953, they redrew the limits of human capability. Hillary's photo of Tenzing on the summit was proof of success and, later, made others wonder if there might be another evidentiary photo lost on Everest. Englishman George Mallory had been carrying a folding Kodak when he and Andrew Irvine were lost near the top in 1924. Were they still on their way up, or coming back down, when they had died? A 1999 U.S. expedition sought the answer and did find Mallory's body—but not his camera.

Photograph by
Sir Edmund Hillary
Royal Geographical Society

Other Landmark Images

Photography is persuasive when you're dealing with a mountaintop, less so as proof of polar conquest. U.S. explorer Robert E. Peary's photo of his happy crew does not prove that he is at the North Pole on April 6, 1909—and, in fact, Peary's claim has been disputed. The picture of Norwegian Roald Amundsen taking a sighting at the South Pole in December 1911 is authentic: A month later, ill-fated Englishman Robert Falcon Scott came upon the flag at precisely 90 degrees south latitude.

The North Pole, 1909
Photograph from
Hulton Archive/Getty

The South Pole, 1911
Photograph by
Bjorn Finstad, Oslo
Courtesy Olav Bjaaland

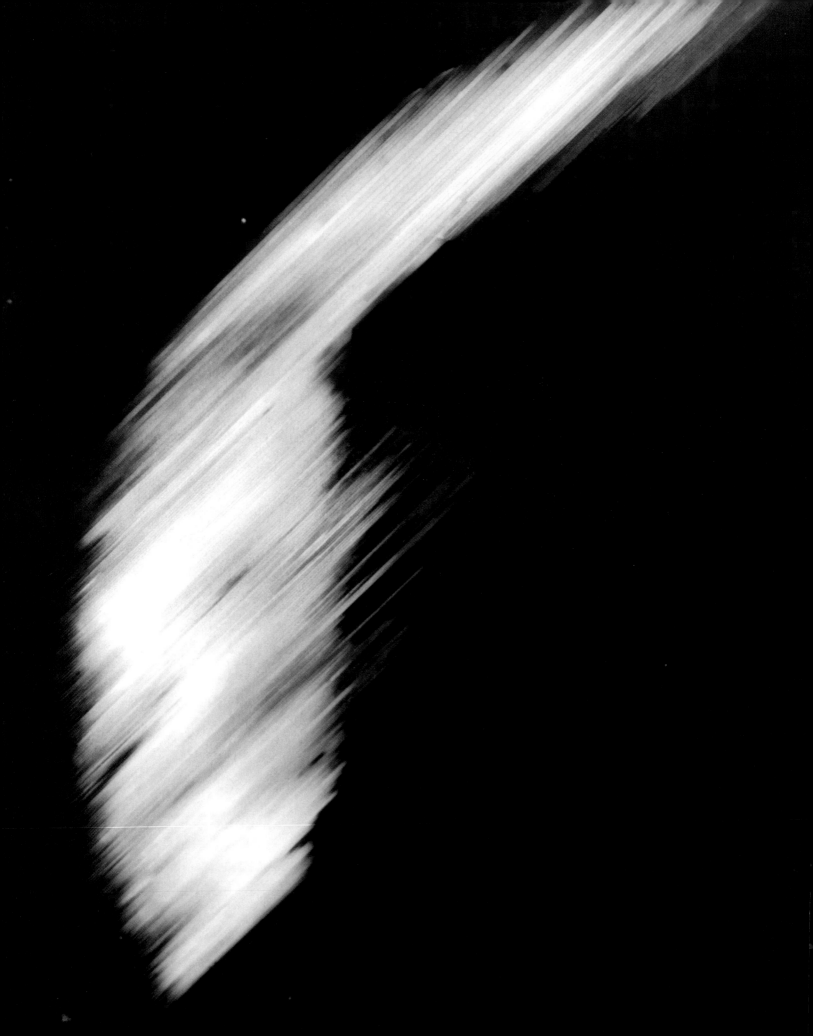

First Human X-ray 1896

To know something like the back of your hand is a timeless concept, one taken yet further by Wilhelm Konrad Roentgen. While working on a series of experiments with a Crookes tube, he noticed that a bit of barium platinocyanide emitted a fluorescent glow. He then laid a photographic plate behind his wife's hand (note the wedding rings), and made the first X-ray photo. Before that, physicians were unable to look inside a person's body without making an incision. Roentgen was the recipient of the first Nobel Prize for Physics in 1901.

Photograph by
Wilhelm Roentgen
Courtesy General Electric Co.

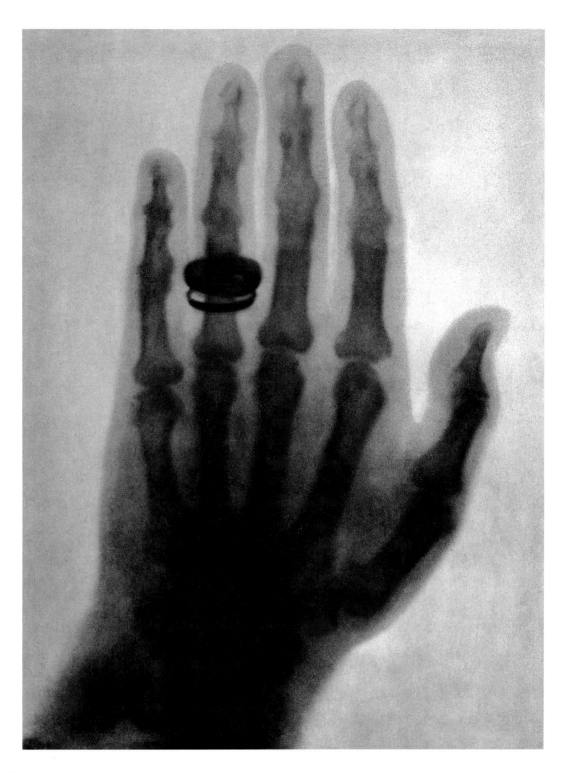

First Satellite Picture 1959

Goaded by the Soviets' successful launch of Sputnik 1 in 1957, America shot its first satellite, Explorer 1, into orbit the next year. The space race was on, and by the time of Explorer 6, NASA was able to get the first image of Earth from a satellite. It was less than revelatory. You would never know it, but this crude blur captured from 17,000 miles above Mexico on August 14, 1959, actually shows sunlight hitting clouds over the central Pacific Ocean. Undeterred, in 1960, NASA launched the Tiros program and proved the technique useful for weather forecasters. Other scientists—and spies—also put space photos to work.

Photograph from NASA

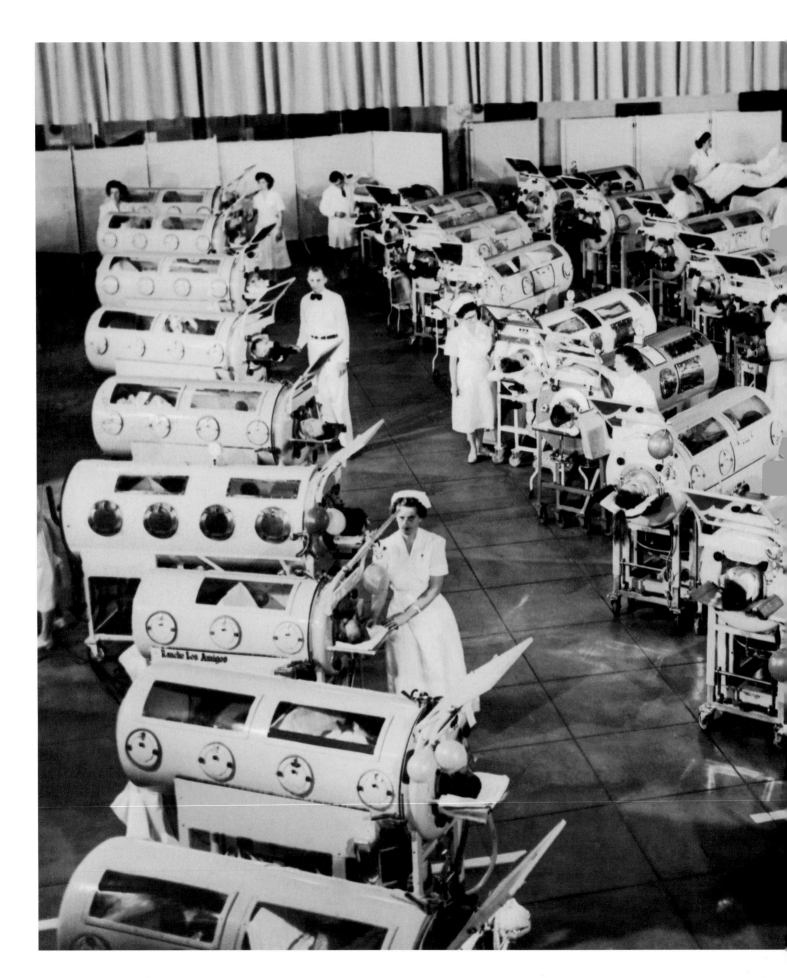

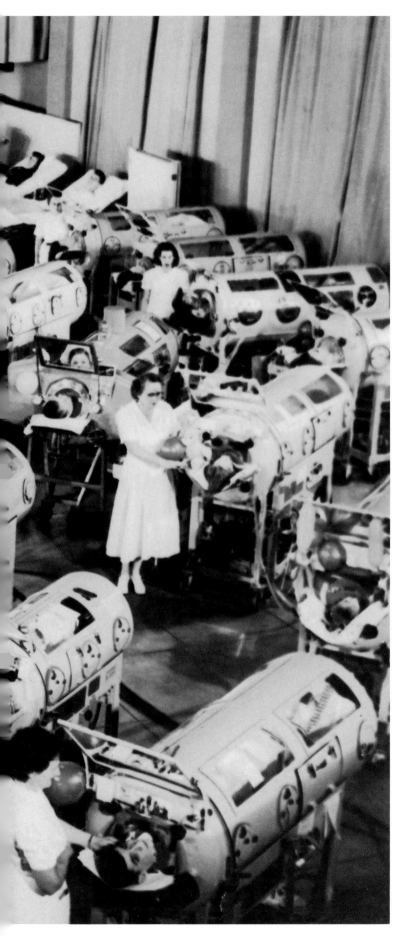

Iron Lung Polio Patients 1950

A monstrous breathing machine aptly called the iron lung was once the only way to keep some polio victims from suffocating. Pictures of kids doomed to the frightening contraptions proved to be very effective in getting people to take safety precautions—and, soon, polio shots. Said Dr. Edward Rothstein, an adviser to the American Academy of Pediatrics, "I remember how the fear of polio changed our lives—not going to the swimming pool in summer, not going to the movies . . . I remember pictures of wards full of iron lungs, hundreds in a room, with kids who couldn't breathe in them. It affected daily life more than AIDS does today." Lacking a similarly repellent photographic image, some parents today eschew vaccination because they think the health risks outweigh benefits.

Photographer Unknown

Thalidomide 1962

A drug called thalidomide was first marketed in Germany in 1957 as a sedative. Tests had been done on the drug, but procedures were not as thorough as today. Believed safe, it was given to pregnant women around the world as a way to contend with morning sickness. Before too long, a terrible development was observed: Babies were being born with pronounced limb deformation. Images of children with abbreviated arms were seen everywhere, but the tragedy that involved some 20,000 children did at least serve to change the way drug information is distributed to governments.

Photograph by **Stan Wayman**

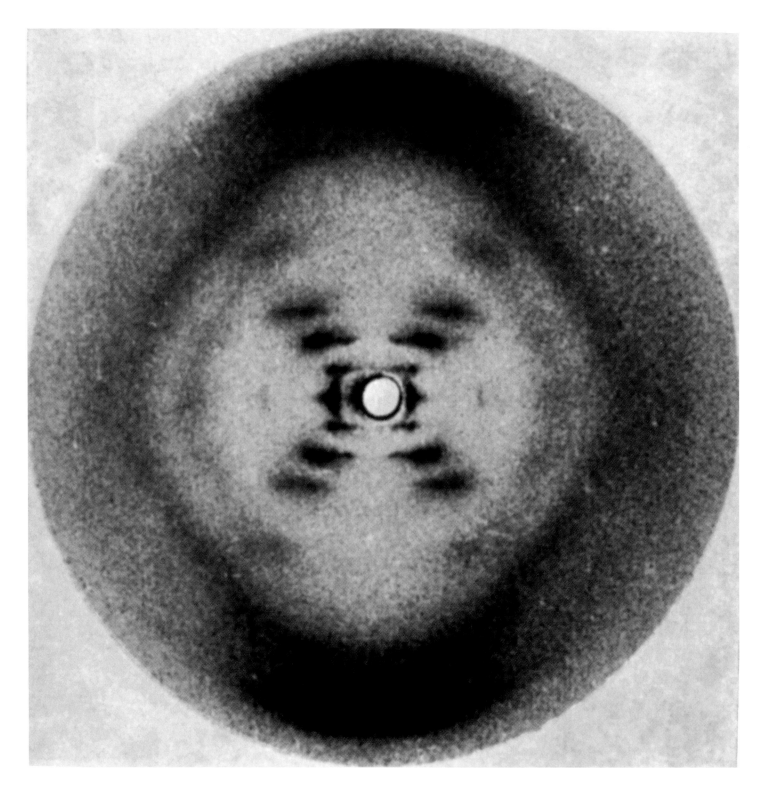

Exposure 51 1952

Scientists were in a heated race in May 1952 to be the first to discover the cellular basis of heredity. At King's College, Rosalind Franklin exposed crystalline strands to 100 hours of radiation in a series of X-rays. Her colleague Maurice Wilkins privately showed her work to molecular biologists James Watson and Francis Crick, who used one X-ray, Exposure 51, to decode the double helix of DNA—the blueprint for all living things. "The instant I saw the picture, my mouth fell open and my pulse began to race," said Watson. In 1958, Franklin died of cancer in relative obscurity—likely from radiation she was exposed to in her work. The three men shared a 1962 Nobel Prize.

Photograph by **Franklin, R. and Gosling, R.G.** Nature

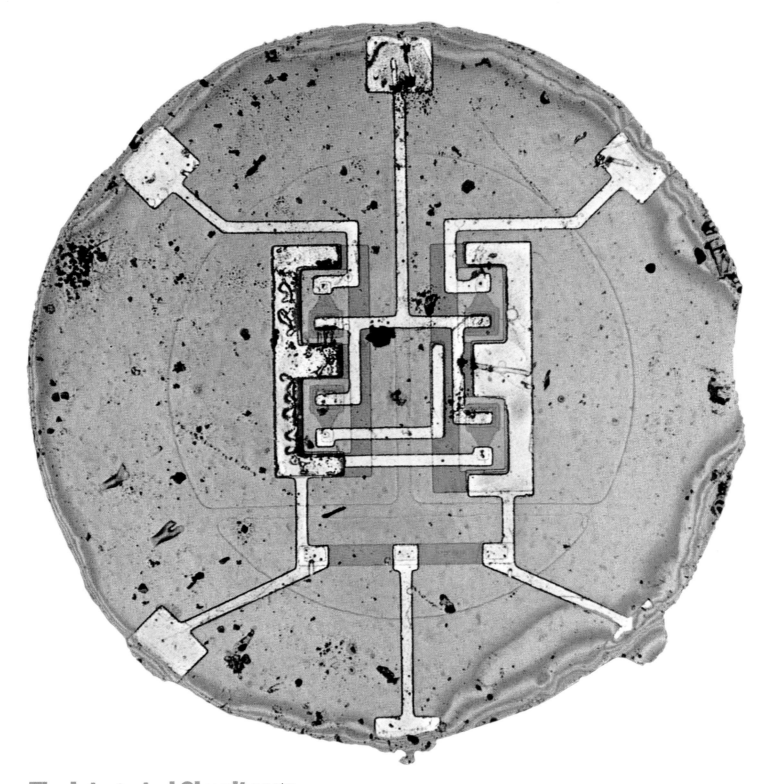

The Integrated Circuit 1959

By the late '50s, electronics was steadily moving from vacuum tubes to transistors, but workers still had to use tweezers to clumsily fashion together wire, transistor, platform and so on. Then, at nearly the same time, two computer-industry inventors, Jack Kilby and Robert Noyce, independently created the IC; Noyce's first circuit was literally photographed onto the chip. Today, 125 million transistors can fit within one square inch, and the computer revolution that evolved from their relatively simple discovery has, for better or worse, permeated every aspect of human existence. Kilby went on to invent the portable calculator, while Noyce cofounded the chip giant Intel.

Photograph by **Robert Noyce** Courtesy Fairchild Semiconductor International

Holography 1948

The Hungarian-born electrical engineer Dennis Gabor was trying to improve electron microscopes when he created a hologram—a photographic recording of an image which organizes light into a three-dimensional representation of the subject. Gabor received the Nobel Prize for Physics in 1971 for his discovery, but it really wasn't until the development of the laser in the early '60s that holography (demonstrated here in 1966) realized its full breadth. Its applications are many, including the detection of structural strain in buildings.

Photograph by **Fritz Goro**

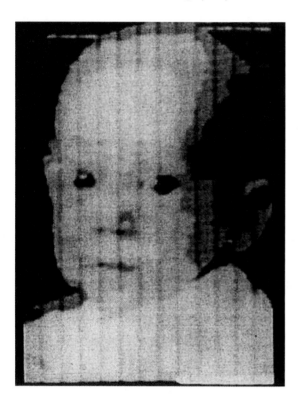

Digital Imaging 1957

The camera and the computer had yet to join forces when Russell Kirsch set out to create the first computerized photo. To achieve this, he invented the photographic scanner as well as computer-imaging software. The first image Kirsch scanned—apparently seeking a Kodak moment—was of his infant son, Walden. It was the initial step toward NASA's planetary pictures and, closer to home, today's increasingly popular digital snapshots.

Binary Scan by **Russell A. Kirsch**
Courtesy Russell A. Kirsch & NIST

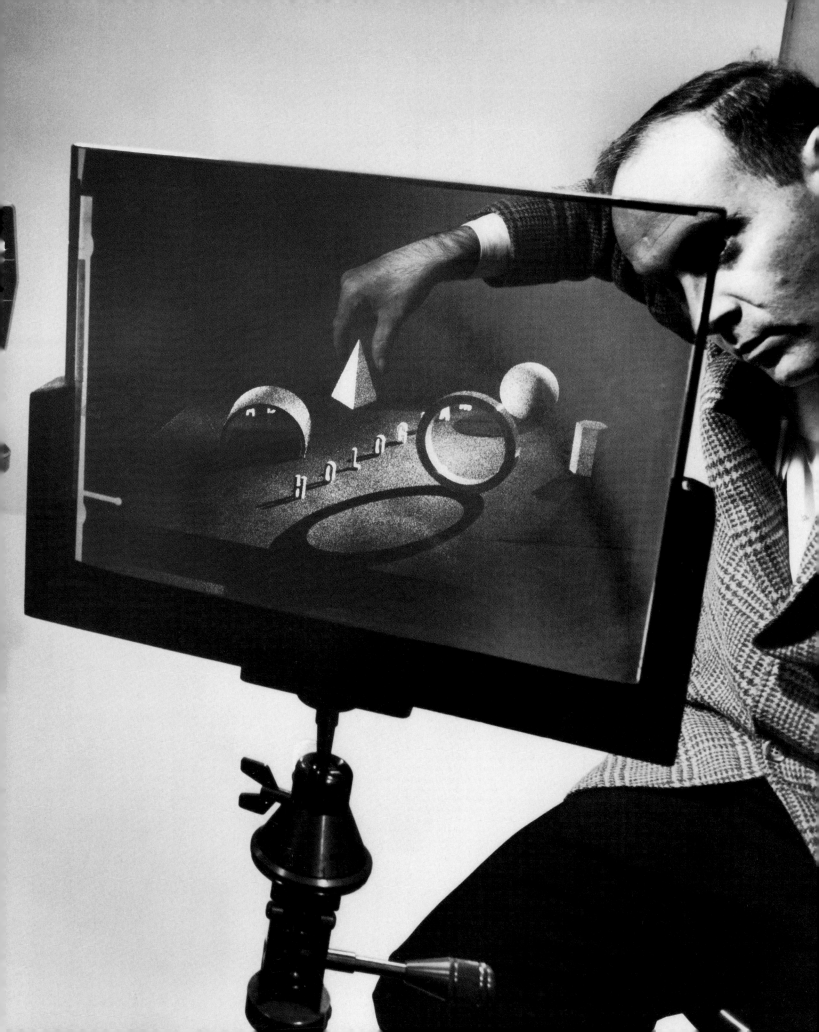

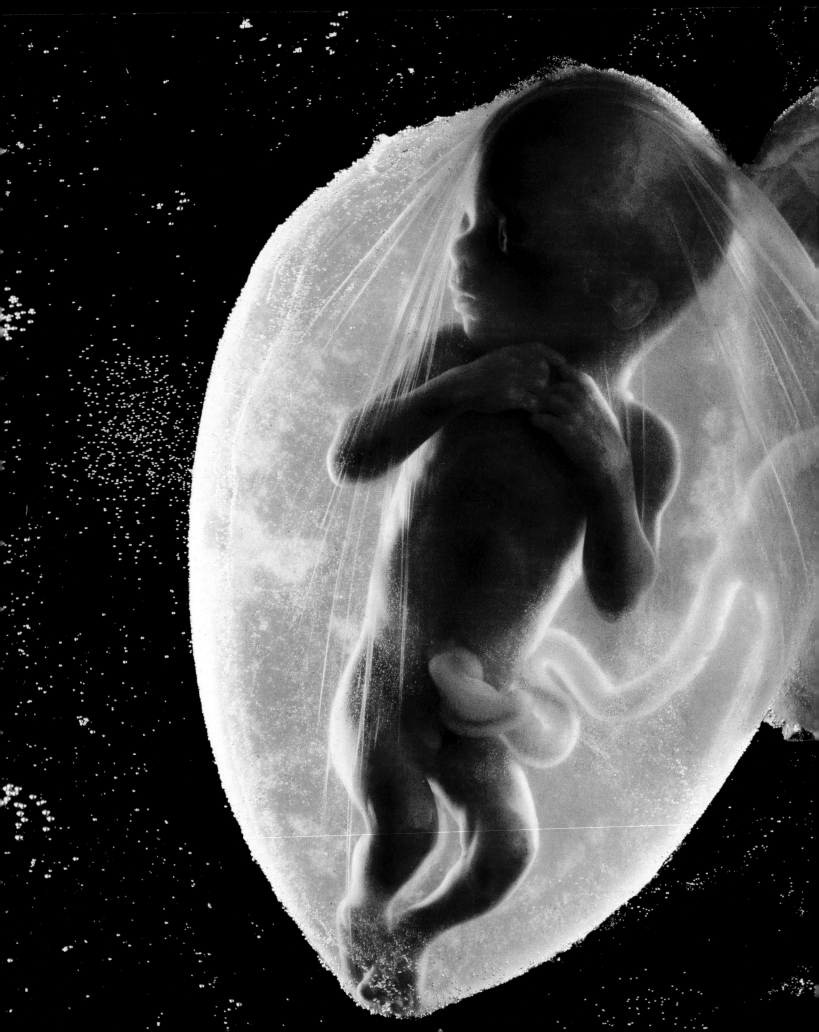

How Life Begins
1965

In 1957 he began taking pictures with an endoscope, an instrument that can see inside a body cavity, but when Lennart Nilsson presented the rewards of his work to LIFE's editors several years later, they demanded that witnesses confirm that they were seeing what they thought they were seeing. Finally convinced, they published a cover story in 1965 that went on for 16 pages, and it created a sensation. Then, and over the intervening years, Nilsson's painstakingly made pictures informed how humanity feels about . . . well, humanity. They also were appropriated for purposes that Nilsson never intended. Nearly as soon as the 1965 portfolio appeared in LIFE, images from it were enlarged by right-to-life activists and pasted to placards.

Photograph by **Lennart Nilsson**

Earthrise 1968

The late adventure photographer Galen Rowell called it "the most influential environmental photograph ever taken." Captured on Christmas Eve, 1968, near the end of one of the most tumultuous years the U.S. had ever known, the Earthrise photograph inspired contemplation of our fragile existence and our place in the cosmos. For years, Frank Borman and Bill Anders of the Apollo 8 mission each thought that he was the one who took the picture. An investigation of two rolls of film seemed to prove Borman had taken an earlier, black-and-white frame, and the iconic color photograph, which later graced a U.S. postage stamp and several book covers, was by Anders.

Photograph by **William Anders** NASA

Another Landmark Image

Neil Armstrong was the first man on the moon in 1969, the one who delivered the memorable words: "One small step for man, one giant leap for mankind." (He later changed this to "One small step for *a* man.") Armstrong was also the guy with the camera, most of the time, and so the best images of *Apollo 11*'s historic mission, including this one, star the second man on the moon, Buzz Aldrin.

Buzz Aldrin, 1969
Photograph by **Neil Armstrong** NASA

Challenger 1986

Having seen 24 space shuttle missions go forth and safely return, Americans were delighted when NASA invited high-school teacher Christa McAuliffe to fly on the next one. The New Hampshirite's son, daughter and students were eagerly watching at Cape Canaveral on the morning of January 28. Delayed seven times, the *Challenger* finally launched at 11:38 a.m. Then, 73 seconds into its flight, the craft disintegrated and swirled into the ocean in a cloud of white vapor. Despite expansive TV coverage, this still photograph became emblematic of a tragedy that saddened so many, and changed their views of space, rekindling the debate about whether man even belonged up there.

Photograph by **Michelle McDonald**

Another Landmark Image

Man has been gazing at Mars for ages: Who or what might be living next door? Well, it turns out, nobody—not these days. But recent pictures beamed back through space have indicated a number of water-source regions on the Red Planet, which of course means that way back when . . . maybe there was . . . perhaps there could have been? This photograph was shot on January 14, 2011, by the High Resolution Imaging Science camera on NASA's Mars Reconnaissance Orbiter, and it shows many channels from one to 10 yards wide in the Hellas impact basin.

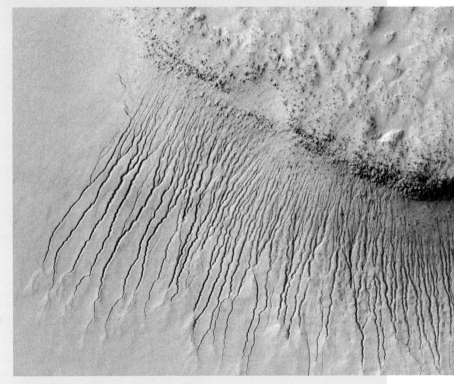

Mars Reconnaissance Orbiter, 2011
Photograph from NASA/JPL/Reuters

P/2010 A2 2010

Our 100th photograph that changed the world may never, in fact, do so, but it is a picture of a world changing and—who knows?—it might be related to one of the most cataclysmic events our green old Earth has ever experienced. In January 2010 the Hubble Space Telescope spotted an object circling about 90 million miles from our planet, in the main asteroid belt between Mars and Jupiter. Astronomers coldly assigned this comet-like spheroid the vigorously unpoetic name P/2010 A2, then puzzled over what the bizarre X-pattern of filamentary structures near the pointed nucleus of the object, and trailing steamers of dust, might signify. Finally, they figured the object was created by a collision of two asteroids, possible siblings of the rogue rock blamed for killing our dinosaurs millions of years ago. Now *that's* changing the world.

Photograph from NASA/Reuters